PRAISE FOR
"LESSONS FROM 90 YEARS OF LIVING"

"Earlier in his life, Jerry Apps met an African woman, a UN delegate, enrolled in his story-telling workshop at the UN building in NYC. She told him how important stories were in her native culture, and stated, in a quiet focused voice, that in America we too often have allowed others to tell our own stories. Profoundly impacted, Jerry, re-committed to telling our own stories as long as he would be able. May we all be so fortunate to have the good fortune to listen to and learn from a kind, decent, wise human being like Jerry Apps: Well, here's our chance. This book is a gift that should be cherished. Thank you, Jerry, from my heart."

—Richard L. Cates, Jr., author of *Voices From the Heart of the Land: A Farm Family's Journey Toward a Land Ethic*

"Jerry Apps has crafted an engaging tour of his life and freely invites us to walk beside him to witness it together. Through the good times, the laughter with family and friends, the humbling moments, and, yes, the disappointments and great personal loss, he accepts it all while conveying an evenness others may find useful in their own lives. He offers a template of tips to consider in helping us find our own resolve – much like he found his – to continue developing a vibrant life regardless of one's age or situation. He brings to us his most poignant and personal story yet, but one filled with hope that will stay with us long after we have turned the last page. This is a gift from a man who has walked many different roads and freely shares what he has learned – always the storyteller and the teacher we have come to know."

—Phil Hasheider, author of 30 books on farming, local history, and family stories.

LESSONS FROM
90 YEARS OF LIVING

LESSONS LEARNED FROM 90 YEARS OF LIVING

JERRY APPS

Milwaukee, Wisconsin

Copyright © 2025 by Jerry Apps
All rights reserved.

Photographs courtesy of the Apps family.
Cover photo by Steve Apps.

Published by
HenschelHAUS Publishing, Inc.
Milwaukee, Wisconsin
www.henschelHAU.S.books.com

ISBN: 979-8992107074
LCCN: 2025932748

Printed in the United States of America.

Dedication

*To my late wife Ruth,
to whom I had been married for 63 years*

Table of Contents

Preface: A Long and Twisting Road i

Part I: Growing Up on a Farm
Chapter 1   The Early Years 3
Chapter 2   Young-Man Lessons 9
Chapter 3   Influence of Place... 17
Chapter 4   One-Room Country School........................... 23
Chapter 5   High School Years.. 27

Part II: College Years
Chapter 6   University of Wisconsin–Madison................. 35
Chapter 7   ROTC... 39
Chapter 8   Summer Work and Campus Jobs 47

Part III: Post-College Years
Chapter 9   First Job after College..................................... 55
Chapter 10 Army Active and Reserve Duty 59
Chapter 11 University of Wisconsin Work 67

Part IV: Early Retirement Years
Chapter 12 Full-Time Writer, Part-Time Teacher............ 73
Chapter 13 The Power of Storytelling 77

Part V: Informal Education
Chapter 14 Libraries and the Internet 83
Chapter 15 Lessons From Nature 87
Chapter 16 Trees I Have Known 97
Chapter 17 Seasonal Change 101
Chapter 18 Music and Movies...107

Part VI: Adjusting to Change
Chapter 19 Religion—Before 1961 115
Chapter 20 Religion—After 1961 123
Chapter 21 Life's Turning Points—The Early Years 131
Chapter 22 Life's Turning Points—The Later Years 137
Chapter 23 Living Through Loss.....................................143

Epilogue 149
Acknowledgments 153
Other Books by Jerry Apps..155

Preface: A Long and Twisting Road

"Two roads diverged in a wood, and I—
I took the one less traveled by,
And that has made all the difference."
—Robert Frost

In our apartment is a wall hanging of a crooked trail in the woods, which disappears with no end in sight. It was given to me by a visiting professor from China, who worked with me one year during the time I taught at the UW-Madison. For me, that trail in the woods is a metaphor for my life.

I have more than three miles of trails at my farm, Roshara, in central Wisconsin. My trails have their ups and downs. Sometimes they go straight ahead for a quarter mile or so and then they make an abrupt turn, as the trail avoids a huge tree in the way. There are lumps and bumps in my life's trails, sometimes the ride over them is downright scary as the trail drops nearly straight down, and a few moments later, turns and goes up, up and more up to a top of a hill where I can see far into the distance.

Many of my trails are those less traveled. Traveling on these trails has an uncanny similarity to the life I have lived these 90 years. I have followed familiar roads, and I have taken many that were less traveled. The end of the road is not yet in sight, a good thing, as I continue to travel along it, wondering when the next bump will come, when the next hill to climb will appear, when the next big tree will loom up in front of me causing me to change direction, and perhaps even cause me to make a new road.

In this book, I will share some of what I consider the important lessons I have learned as I have traveled the roads of my life and have confronted the good and the bad, the exciting and the boring, the life threatening and the life enhancing.

Some years ago, when I was working on one of my books about farm life, I interviewed a fellow who must have been close to the age I am now. As I was prone to do, and continue to do now, is to ask what some of my interviewees see as strange questions. My question to this fellow: "What would you say about the life you have so far lived?"

His answer, "I was born with nothing and I have most of it left." I suspect he was pulling my leg and probably only thinking about material things such as money saved, property owned and stuff accumulated. I have never forgotten the words he spoke. And I wondered how many people believed they ended up with what they born with—nothing. For me, it is not the materialistic that made a difference in my life--it is important to have a roof over your head, enough to eat, and as I got older good medical services. But beyond these basics, what I have learned beyond the materialistic has made all the difference. My life's road has not always been bathed in sunshine and cool breezes, but I have so much to be thankful for.

My father had little formal education—he completed fifth grade—but he was a man of wisdom and a great storyteller. With his passing at age 93, I wrote across the top of a page in my journal, "Things I learned from my father." It was my way of grieving my loss. I thought I would fill up a couple of pages with my memories.

As it turned out, a book resulted from this effort. (*Rural Wit and Wisdom: Time-Honored Values From the Midwest*, Fulcrum Press). Some of these lessons are included in this book. I have also drawn on my memories, many of which are as vivid as when the events happened. I've also taken material from a daily journal I have written nearly every day for more than fifty years. On these pages, I will take you, the reader, on a trip along the

Preface

roads of my life, on both the roads most traveled, and many that were not. And, as I am now in the autumn of my life, here are some lessons I have learned along the way that may be useful to you.

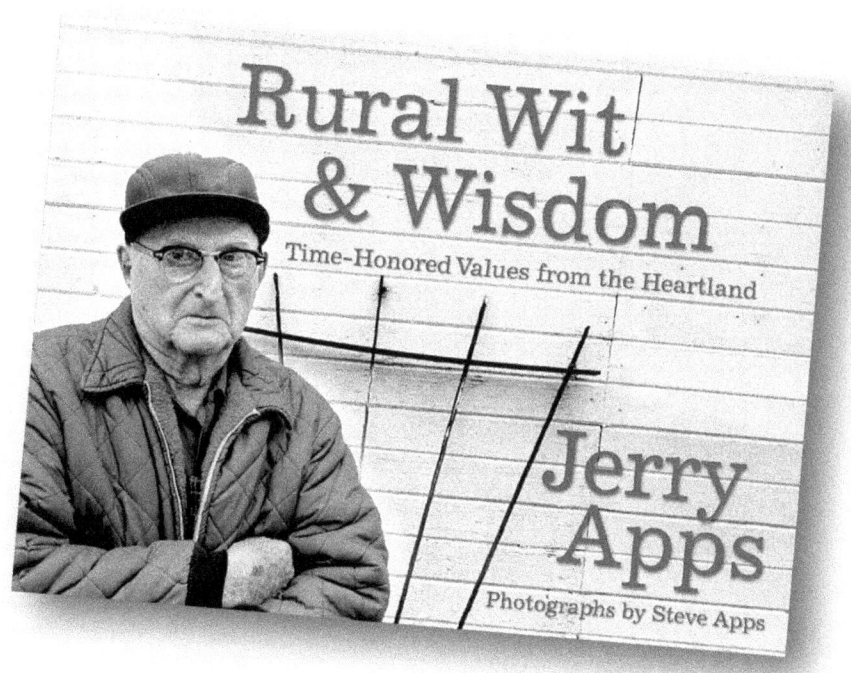

Part I
Growing Up on a Farm

I was born July 25, 1934.

Chapter 1
The Early Years

We had no electricity, no indoor plumbing and heated our drafty farmhouse with woodstoves. No one knew there was such a thing as air-conditioning. We did have a party-line telephone, and my mother alerted Dr. Karnup in Wautoma when I was on the way. Wautoma was about 12 miles from our farm. Our nearby neighbors to the south were the Millers—farmers like we were. Mrs. Miller was a midwife for the community as well. As my mother related, Mrs. Miller had come shortly after the phone call. And some time later, I don't have the exact time, I came into this world.

I was born on July 25, 1934, in a farmhouse located in the township of Rose, Waushara County, Wisconsin. My arrival was a bit of a surprise, as my parents, Herman and Eleanor Apps, had been married ten years before I was born. Years later, my parents told me about that hot day in July, when Pa was busy preparing our grain crop for the threshing crew that was to arrive in a few days, and how I had interrupted those plans.

In those days, farm kids were born at home as the nearest hospital was forty miles away (Stevens Point). In 1934, the country was deep in the Great Depression. Unemployment had reached 25 percent. To add to the misery, a drought had settled over the southwestern states, with high winds causing roaring dust storms. Farm people suffered from the Depression with low prices for farm products. Farmers suffered, along with everyone else, from the malaise that had settled over the country. My parents were renting the home farm at the time, and struggled to make enough money to make the farm rental payments. Almost all farmers were in dire straits as the Great Depression that had begun in 1929, continued, year after year, until the Second World War, which began December 7, 1941.

Many people, especially those living in urban areas, were not only without employment, but were without food and housing. I don't ever remember going hungry and I always had a roof over my head. Ma tended a large vegetable garden, as well as looked after a flock of laying hens, usually a hundred or more. She traded the eggs for groceries at the Wild Rose Mercantile. With meat from a hog we butchered each fall, and the garden produce we ate fresh in the summer and from canning of vegetables and fruits my ma prepared for winter, we were mostly self-sufficient. The groceries from town were bare minimum. As I remember, those were sugar, salt, coffee—the basics that we could not produce on the farm. Eggs also paid for the clothes that my brothers and I wore, such as bib overalls a couple pair of new ones each year, and several new shirts—and shoes for kids' feet that were forever growing larger.

I was learning how to grow the family's food, and the importance of providing one's own food. I was learning to help in the garden when I was just a little guy—everyone helped out in the garden at one time or another.

Pa's small herd of dairy cows provided us with milk, butter, and cheese, and a regular income to cover the general cost of operating the farm: the milling costs for grinding oats and corn for cattle feed, monthly rent for the farm, that sort of thing.

During the years that I was growing up on our 160-acre farm, no one had to travel to work, different from urban families. We lived in the midst of our work and we never left it. The chickens and hogs had to be fed each day. The dairy cows had to be milked and fed each day. Those were our chores. No one talked about doing them; no one complained about doing them. They were just done. They were an important part of what it meant to live on a family farm. The lessons I was learning were many, though I didn't realize I was learning them.

My first memories of a family lesson I was aware of occurred when I was maybe three years old. I was old enough to explore and curious enough to want to do it. I began to discover that a farm, especially one that was 160 acres with both open fields for farming, and a 20-acre woodlot was a wonderful place to explore. It must have been the fall of 1937 when I got my first strong lesson related to my exploring and not telling anyone what I was doing or where I was doing it.

Pa, in addition to having a small herd of dairy cows, grew 20 acres of potatoes at the time. The potato crop was one source of extra income for the farm. In 1937, the potato field was located in the southwest corner of the farm, a good half mile or more from the farm buildings. At the time, I had a toy wheelbarrow, and in it I had a Teddy Bear that I took everywhere with me. A wagon trail led from the farm buildings to the potato field. Pa followed the trail several days in fall with our team of horses, a steel-wheeled wagon, and a goodly number of wooden bushel potato crates.

On a clear, sunny October morning, I decided to follow the wagon trail to the potato field to see where it went. I did not know that at the time, it led to the potato patch where Pa was working. At age three, I had no sense of time, so I had no idea how long it took me with my little short legs and a wheelbarrow, to walk a half mile along the wagon trail on the way to where I did not know. I was learning the fun of exploration. But I had no idea of the consequences of what I was doing.

Finally, I could see Pa in the distance; he seemed to be digging with a fork, but I couldn't see why he was doing that. When he saw me, he dropped the fork and ran to me. "What are you doing here?" he said, with a serious tone to his voice. "Did your ma know where you were going?"

I was surprised to see him, as he was unhappily surprised to see me.

— 5 —

"What are you doing?" I asked, looking at the fork a few feet away.

"Digging potatoes," Pa said.

"What's that?" I asked.

He took the fork, stuck it into the ground near a little brown, bushy plant, dug up the plant, and several big, white potatoes rolled out on the ground. I was amazed to find out where potatoes came from, but I did not think about the consequences to what I had done—walked a half mile out to the potato patch with my wheelbarrow and Teddy Bear.

Pa dug his pocket watch out of his bib overalls, checked the time, and said, "Almost time for supper. You can help me pick up the potatoes."

With the potatoes gathered and the boxes loaded on the wagon, Pa loaded me, my wheelbarrow, and my Teddy Bear on the wagon and we started along the wagon trail for home. What fun it was to ride on the wagon with Pa. It was the first time I remember doing that.

Soon we arrived at home. I saw Ma standing on the farmhouse porch. She looked like she had been crying. She also looked angry. She ran out to the wagon and grabbed me off of it.

"Where have you been?" she asked with a loud voice.

"Helping Pa with the potatoes," I said, smiling.

"You what?" Ma asked. "You're too little to help pick potatoes."

"But that's what I did," I said, still smiling.

"He's okay. He walked out to see me," Pa said, trying to save me from more verbal punishment.

Our basic farm family included Ma, Pa, me, and my twin brothers, Donald and Darrel, who were born on January 31, 1938. But there were more members as well—at least we considered them part of the family. Our farm dog, Fanny, was clearly a part of the family. This may be a stretch, but Pa would not say it was. Our small herd of Holstein milk cows was a part of the family. They were named after women that Pa and Ma knew in the community: Mable, Lucy, Margaret, and so on. Why were the cows a part of the family? As I think back to those early years—indeed all of my growing-up years—the cows were the center of our attention—we milked them twice a day, 365 days of the year. No vacations. Not only did each cow have a name, she had a personality, she had a way of doing things, she liked being milked or she didn't. Pa knew all of this, of course.

I was learning these lessons without realizing it. As I think back to those growing-up years, so much of what I learned was not in the textbooks I later would study.

Back to the dairy cows and their personalities. When I was ten years old or so, I sometimes had the task of "fetching the cows"— Pa's words for asking me to walk out to the pasture with our dog Fanny and bring the cows home for milking. Fanny and I would walk along the lane for a quarter mile or so to where the cattle were eating and resting in the night pasture. Fanny walked among the resting cows, barked a couple of times until one of the cows got up, and then Fanny moved on to the next one. It was at these times I saw the relationship that Fanny had with the cows—especially the boss cow. Yes, there was a boss cow who always led the string of cows down the dusty lane to the barn for the morning milking. Fanny and I walked at the end of the string of cows. I was too young to realize that the boss cow and Fanny were really taking care of the situation.

Fanny was a Collie; she was a working dog and not a pet. Fanny was not allowed in the house except on cold winter days, when she slept in front of the wood-burning cook stove in the kitchen. The rest of the time, she slept on a rug on the kitchen porch. One of her roles was that of watch dog. She was aware of a raccoon, or weasel, or some other animal looking to make a meal of one of our chickens in the dead of night. A few barks and growls and the chickens were saved. When a traveling salesman drove into the yard, Fanny was the first to greet him with her barking. Her greeting turned some unknowing salesmen away without ever opening their car door to greet Fanny, who really was quite friendly.

Fanny also was a "kid protector." If one of my brothers or I wandered down to the country road that passed by our farm, she was there to push us back, to keep us safe.

Lessons

- Appreciate what you have, although it may be little.
- Appreciate the importance of a loving family.
- Don't go anywhere without telling your mother where you are going.
- Animals can become friends.
- Learn how to grow vegetables in a garden.
- You gain important lessons without realizing you are learning them.

Chapter 2
Young-Man Lessons

I often heard the following words from Pa, "Do the best you can with what you've got."

Especially I heard this when I said, "I don't think I can do that." I've tried to follow Pa's advice my entire life. Now that I am in my 90s, those words continue to resonate with me.

Once I reached age 14, I was able to "work out," which meant I could be hired by a neighbor to help him make hay or do some other job. Payment was a dollar a day, plus lunch.

Starting in late June and continuing into July, each year we made hay. The task was not easy but it was necessary. With the barn loft filled with hay, we could feed the cattle and horses through our long, cold Wisconsin winters. Pa would keep careful watch of the hayfield, where brome grass, red clover, and alfalfa grew. Generally, we had 20 acres of hay. When Pa decided the hay was ready for cutting, usually on a bright, sunny day in June, he would hitch the team to our five-foot mower and begin cutting the hay. Around and around the field he drove, usually taking a day or more to complete the cutting.

We hoped for several days of sunny warm weather so the cut hay would dry. Pa, and often with me along, would go out to the field several times to see how the drying was progressing. When he deemed the hay ready, he hitched our horses Frank and Charlie to the hay rake, and once more, he drove around and around the field, raking the freshly cut hay into long ropes, maybe a foot or two tall.

Then it was time for me to appear with my three-tine hay fork. I bunched the raked hay into little piles that were three to four feet tall. Pa showed me how to rake the hay in bunches so that they would shed a light rain.

When Pa deemed the hay dry enough, he hitched the team to the steel-wheeled hay wagon. We pitched the hay onto the wagon and hauled it to the barn. Using a series of pullies and a heavy hayfork rope, the loose hay was hauled up into the haymows by a horse hitched to the heavy rope. One person set the hayfork on the load of hay, and a second person worked in the haymow, pitching back the hay. It was extremely important that the hay was properly dried. If it wasn't, it might spontaneously combust, meaning it would catch fire and the barn would burn. Almost every summer, we'd hear of someone's barn burning because the hay hadn't dried enough.

Not long after the haying season was over, the oat crop ripened and was ready for cutting with our grain binder, a machine that cut the grain and formed it into little bundles as the team of horses pulled the machine around the oat field. My job was to stand the bundles into oat shocks, five pairs of bundles in each shock, and placed so they were sturdy enough to withstand a stiff wind and a driving rain. Pa helped once the field was cut.

A week or so later, the grain was ready for threshing. A threshing machine, sometimes owned by one of the farmers in the neighborhood, made its way from farm to farm, threshing the grain—removing the oat kernels from their stalks and blowing the yellow straw into huge straw stacks, which usually stood near the barn.

By age 14, I was old enough to drive our tractor on a bundle wagon and haul wagonloads of bundles to the threshing machine. Once there, I tossed the bundles into the little elevator that pulled the bundles into the machine. It was hard, dusty work, but I was proud that I was able to do it.

By working on a threshing crew, I got to know our neighbors—their troubles, and their hopes. I learned their work skills.

YOUNG-MAN LESSONS

My mother made a Teddy bear for me out of a feed sack.

Some were really good at the various tasks associated with threshing, others less so. I learned not to be critical of those who I believed were not working as well as I thought they should. I learned about the cooking skills of the neighbor women, most of whom I would give an A rating, a few less so.

In the 1930s and 1940s, we planted 20 acres of potatoes, sometimes more. We planted them by hand, cultivated them with a one-horse walking cultivator, and spent untold hours hoeing out the weeds the cultivator missed. Come October and potato harvest time, our country school, along with all the country schools in central Wisconsin closed for two weeks for "potato vacation." Some vacation! Every chilly vacation day morning, we loaded wooden potato crates on our steel-wheeled, horse-drawn wagon.

We distributed the potato crates every few yards across the field, and Pa and a hired man began digging. Each used a six-tine barn fork and backed their way across the field, each digging two rows while my two brothers and I scrambled to pick the big white potatoes and drop them into pails. When those were full, we dumped the spuds into the potato boxes. It was back-breaking work, but the smells of new potatoes and freshly turned soil were pleasant ones.

Besides that, we earned a handsome one cent a bushel for the potatoes we picked, more than most of the kids in the neighborhood who received no pay whatever for their efforts. I purchased my first .22 rifle with potato-picking money.

By late October, the corn crop was ready for harvest. We grew 20 to 25 acres of corn. Pa cut the standing corn with a corn binder pulled by our team of horses. Once cut, Pa, my brothers, and I stood the corn bundles into corn shocks that marched across the cornfield.

After a few weeks, a corn-husking machine arrived at the farm, a smaller version of a threshing machine. The corn husker removed the ears of corn from the stalks, and the husks from the ears. It then cut up the stalks, which were blown into our barn for later use as bedding for our cows. The yellow ears of husked corn tumbled into a wagon. When the wagon was full, we forked the cobs into the corn crib.

Corn husking involved several of the neighbors, just as threshing. It took a couple of weeks for the corn husker to make the rounds of the neighbors, tending to each farmer's corn crop, and leaving the corn fields with rows of corn stubble. With good fall weather, the naked corn fields were plowed down in preparation for the following year's oat crop. No successive crops of corn on the same field, which is often the case today.

* * *

We heated our drafty farmhouse with woodstoves, one in the kitchen and one in the dining room. We also kept the milk from freezing with a woodstove in the pump house. And the years that

YOUNG-MAN LESSONS

Brothers Darrel, Jerry (with glasses), and Donald, and our parents, Eleanor and Herman Apps. This photo was taken at my parents' 40th wedding anniversary party in 1963.

we raised potatoes as a cash crop, we kept a fire burning in the potato cellar woodstove. We sawed down huge old dead oaks in the woodlot back of the farmstead with a two-man crosscut saw; there were no chainsaws in those days. With the horses and a bob-sleigh, we hauled the limbs and tree trunks to the farmstead and piled them in tall stacks. It was hard, dangerous work.

When this part of the work was completed, we invited the neighbors for a wood-sawing bee. One of neighbors had a power-driven circle saw, which sliced the limbs and trunks into blocks of wood of a manageable size. A reminder of threshing, silo-filling and corn-shredding when the neighbors helped each other. But the work was not done when the neighbors left, for the blocks of wood had to be split into pieces that would fit in the kitchen stove, in the dining room heater, in the pump house stove, and in the potato cellar wood burner that kept our potato crop from freezing.

"Read the wood," Pa would say when we were splitting huge blocks of oak wood and my splitting maul would stick in the block. It was usually this time of the year and more times throughout the late fall and winter that we spent many hours splitting wood for the ever-hungry woodstoves that seemed to always call for more wood.

"Read the wood" meant to study the block before taking a swing at it, looking for the direction of the grain and checking for any knots. A few seconds of study saved several minutes of embarrassment as I tried to extract the splitting maul from a block that I had not read—or had read incorrectly.

Pa made a distinction between work and chores. Work was something that you did once a year, such as making hay. Chores were something that you did every day. Chores, for a farm kid growing up during the Great Depression and World War II, began when I was able to carry split wood from the woodshed to the wood box that stood by the wood-burning kitchen stove in the kitchen. I was about three or four years old when this was my task on the home farm. For Pa, hauling in wood from the wood shed to the kitchen was a chore.

As I remember, it seemed the wood box was always empty, and the words, "Jerold, fetch some more wood" seemed to ring in my ears all day long. Chores included feeding and milking the cows. Feeding the chickens and gathering the eggs. Feeding the pigs and giving them water. And in winter, several additional chores—shoveling the snow from the driveway. Keeping the fires going in the pump house and potato cellar. Removing the manure from behind the cows. Shoveling paths from the farmhouse to the other farm buildings, chicken house, granary, barn, and pump house.

By the time I was five, and in first grade at the Chain O' Lake one-room country school—there was no kindergarten—I had graduated to doing barn chores such as helping feed the calves, and feeding the chickens and the pigs. As I got older, I graduated to more difficult chores, like carrying in straw from the straw stack, and tossing down hay from the haymow.

Lessons

- How to work with neighbors as a team.
- How to work at a job until it is finished.
- How important work is in life.
- How to read a block of wood before splitting it.

The home farm in Waushara County, where I was born and raised.

CHAPTER 3
THE INFLUENCE OF PLACE

Whether we realize it nor not, the place or places where we grew up have and continue to have an influence on who we are today, often when we are not even aware of it. Many of the early lessons we learned have their roots in the home place. Here are some of my early memories of the place where I was born and lived until I was 16 years old and began college at the University of Wisconsin in Madison.

As mentioned earlier. I was born in 1934 on a 160-acre dairy farm in the Town of Rose, Waushara County, Wisconsin. The farm was located four and one-half miles from the village of Wild Rose. I always assumed that the township and nearby village were named after the wild rose, a native wild flower, which grew on our farm, as well as on many of the neighbor farms.

In 1973, I wrote a book titled *Village of Roses, the History of Wild Rose* (available from Wild Rose Historical Society). While writing the book, I searched for the source of the village's name. The obvious answer: it was named after the wild roses growing in the area. Nope, that's not correct. Another possibility, an old-timer shared with a grin on his face. "The village is named after a young lady, Rose. She was a bit on the wild side." Interesting idea, but also not correct.

With a little more digging, I learned that many folks who settled in and around Wild Rose came from upstate New York, from a village named Rose, in Wayne County. It just happened that the year I wrote the book, *Village of Roses*, I also was doing some research at Syracuse University. I looked at a map and discovered Rose was only about an hour's drive from Syracuse, so I drove up there. I stopped at the post office and introduced myself to the elderly clerk as being from Wild Rose, Wisconsin. She greeted me like a long-lost son had returned. I soon discovered that several of the names receiving mail from the post office were the same names as people living in the Wild Rose, Wisconsin area. The man who had homesteaded my farm in 1867, Tom Stewart, came from Rose, New York. A surprising finding, I later learned that Rose, New York, was named after Robert Rose, an early landowner in the town, not after a flower.

* * *

On the home farm, 80 acres were located on each side of the dusty road that trailed past the place. Four 20-acre fields were located on the east side of the road. Various fields, including a 20-acre woodlot, were located on the west side of the road, along with a couple of acres where the farm buildings were located. Our farm crops were rotated on the 20 acres on the east side of the road and a 30-acre field on the west side of the road. The rotation worked like this. One year for corn, the following year for oats, the third year for alfalfa and clover hay, the fourth and fifth years for pasture, then corn again. In this way, weeds could be controlled, land erosion kept at minimum, and soil fertility maintained. It was how we were taking care of the land.

The farm buildings included a barn on the south side of the farmstead, where the cattle were milked, fed, and otherwise cared for. Our team of horses, as well as the calves, were also housed in the barn. To the west of the barn was the brooder house, where little chicks were raised until they were old enough to move to the chicken house, which was on the north side of the property. A wagon shed, corn crib, and granary with machine sheds on either side of it, was located on the west side of the farmstead. The combination pump house and car garage was on the east side of the farmstead. And on the northeast corner of the property was the farmhouse.

The Influence of Place

Each of these buildings has a story to tell, especially the barn where I spent many hours milking cows twice a day and feeding and otherwise caring for them. The farmhouse, on the northeast corner of the farmstead, along with the barn, were the center pieces of the property. As was the custom at the time, all the farm buildings were painted red, except for the farmhouse, which was painted white.

The farmhouse, built about 1900, was not insulated. It had a kitchen, dining room, two bedrooms, and a parlor (living room) on the first floor. It had three bedrooms on the second floor. There was no bathroom as we had no running water. Nor did we have electricity until I was in high school.

In early November, Pa closed off most of the house as it had no central heating. The house had a wood-burning cook stove in the kitchen and a Round Oak, wood-burning stove in the dining room. The only rooms heated were the kitchen, dining room, and one downstairs bedroom. The upstairs bedroom, where my brothers and I slept, had indirect heat—the stove pipe from the dining room stove thrust through our bedroom and into the brick chimney.

In winter, when the fires in the stoves went out around midnight, a great chill came over the house, especially if the outside temperature dipped below zero. Frost covered the inside of our upstairs bedroom windows, so much that we couldn't see outside. Being the oldest, I had to get up at 5:30 for the morning milking. I would grab my clothes and rush down the frigid hallway, and down the stairs to dress in front of the woodstove that Pa started before leaving for the barn. I didn't warm up until I arrived in the barn, where it was always warm.

Electricity didn't come to our farm until the spring of 1947 when I was in eighth grade. By that time, I had grown quite accustomed to lamps and lanterns. Before electricity arrived, we lit our home with kerosene lamps—one in the kitchen and one in the dining room. We used lanterns to light our way in the barn and other outbuildings.

Lessons from 90 Years of Living

The residents of Wild Rose got electricity in 1908. Wild Rose had a water-powered grist mill, which not only ground grain for cattle feed but also powered a generator that provided electricity for the village. In those days, the village people had electricity from sundown until 11 o' clock in the evening. The miller said he needed the waterpower for grinding grain at the mill during the daylight hours. Besides, why would anyone want electricity in the daytime?

Farmers have long been known, especially by their city cousins, as being independent, living far apart from each other, self-sufficient, and not much involved with their neighbors. True, during the years when I was growing up on the home farm (1934-1951), we could only see one of our neighbors from our front porch. The Bill Millers lived more than a half mile to the south of us. A mile away to the south was McKinley Jenks. A quarter mile east of the Jenks farm was Jesse DeWitt's place. Going north of our farmstead to another country road, and then west, lived Andrew Nelson, and across from him Charlie George. Just to the north, on another country road, lived Albert Davis. Another half mile west was Frank Kolka and across from him, Bill Witt, my grandfather. Allen Davis lived north of our farm, about a half mile away and Griff Davis lived east of our farm, with Ed Handrich living across the road from Griff. I may have missed some, but this was our farm community when I was growing up. We knew them well, we knew their dogs' names, knew their horses' names. Of course, we knew their kids' names as we went to country school with them.

Our city cousins were wrong about our independence. True, our immediate family—for me, Pa. Ma, and two brothers—were a unit. We raised most of own food. We worked together as a family, played together, and learned much from each other. But we also interacted with our neighbors, some of them living more than two miles from our farm, As a community, we worked together and played together. This provided me with many lessons on the importance of community, and how much can be learned by interacting with neighbors and helping each other during good times and bad.

Lessons

- The more we know about something, the more likely we are to take care of it.
- Care for the land, as the land cares for us.
- Working as a community is important for a farmer's success.

I attended the Chain O' Lake one-room school for eight years.

Chapter 4
One-Room Country School

Our neighborhood country school had all eight grades in one room with one teacher. There was no kindergarten. The school was named Chain O' Lake for the small lake that was a quarter of a mile to the south of the school.

When I was three years old, I remember waiting at the end of our farm driveway for the neighbor students who walked by our farm each morning and afternoon on their way to school and their way home. I remember the Korleski kids and the Hudziak kids. They always stopped to talk with me; I enjoyed talking with them. Sometimes one of them gave me a cookie from his lunch pail. I couldn't wait to join them on their trip to our school. The Korleski kids had already walked a mile before they got to our farm, with another mile to go. In those days, 1937, there were no school buses.

I turned five years old in July of 1939, and my mother decided I was old enough to go to school. I didn't argue with her. I had been looking forward to it for a long time. I had twin brothers, three and half years old. As I think back to those busy years, I'm sure my mother was pleased that I was off to school. I wore new bib overalls, a new shirt, and my special "go to town" cap. And I combed my hair. Ma said I could not go to school without combing my hair. I hated combing my hair, but I didn't want to get in trouble with Ma, especially not on my first day of school.

I will never forget that late August day in 1939, when the neighbor kids came walking from the north and I joined them on their hike to school. I was a short-legged little guy at the time, and could not walk as fast as the older students, but they didn't mind slowing down so I could keep up. I stood with my lard pail lunch bucket, two new yellow number two pencils, and a five-cent pad of writing paper, waiting for Mike Korleski and the other students. Finally, they appeared and we began walking toward the school.

Elderberries hung heavy along the dusty country road, which was heavily shaded with elm and oak trees. As we walked along, we watched a squirrel scamper up an oak tree. We saw the yellow heads of the goldenrods hanging over the road. Mike was more interested in these things than I was. My thoughts were all about school and what it would be like. What other kids would I meet? Would I be able to learn all that kids were supposed to learn?

When we reached the top of Miller's Hill, we all stopped and listened to the school bell. The teacher rang it at 8:30 each morning. The sound of the bell echoed down the valley where the school was located. Mike said, "We've got a half hour to get to school. Should make it easy."

And we did.

Arriving at the schoolhouse, Mike pulled open the heavy schoolhouse door for me and I entered. My life would be changed forever. Mike introduced me to our teacher, Miss Piechowski, who showed me where my seat was in the front of the room. I was excited, but also a little scared. What would the other kids think of me—I was just a little guy? And I was shy, very shy. I didn't know how to read, knew nothing of arithmetic, and couldn't even write my name.

Mike took me outside and pointed to the two outhouses, one sitting on each corner of the schoolyard—boys on the south side of the yard, girls on the north side. The school had no indoor plumbing, no electricity, and was heated with a woodstove. The same situation we had at home.

Mike and I walked past the combination woodshed-pump house building to the softball diamond.

"Do you know how to play softball?" Mike asked.

"No," I answered.

"I'll show you how," Mike said. He explained where the three bases were—fellow students were standing by each one. Three more students were in back of the diamond. "That's called the outfield," said Mike

Another kid was standing next to home plate—didn't look like a plate to me but that's what Mike called it. Soon, several other kids arrived, school began promptly at 9:00, but we had a few minutes for Mike and the other older kids to show me how to play softball. I quickly learned how to hold a bat, and how to swing at it when a ball went sailing over the plate. I learned that I got three strikes, and if I missed the ball three times, I was out.

* * *

I soon discovered that I loved school because it was there that I learned how to read and appreciate the importance of books. It was there that I learned how to spell, and how to take apart sentences and put them together again. It was there that I learned that 12 x 12 equaled 144, and that the capitol of Ohio was Columbus. And it was there that I learned how to get along with English kids, Polish kids, Bohemian kids, German kids, Norwegian kids, Catholic kids, Baptist kids, Methodist kids, and kids who had never seen the inside of a church. It was there that I spent eight years and developed a great love for reading, for books, and for writing. There was no kindergarten, so I was destined for first grade.

I will never forget that first morning. After my softball lesson, we all filed into the school. Miss Piechowski said "Good morning," and welcomed everybody back to school. Then she introduced Norman Hudziak and me as new first graders. She said we should all go outside and gather around the flag pole. Once there, an eighth grader who was responsible for raising and lowering the flag, did his job as we all recited the *Pledge of Allegiance*. I attended the school for eight years, graduating in 1947, two years after the end of World War II.

Lessons from 90 Years of Living

The Chain O' Lake school closed in 1956. I was in the audience when the families in the Chain O' Lake school district gathered to hear a researcher from Madison explain that all the students in the district—all farm kids—would benefit by attending the consolidated school in Wild Rose. He was there to convince the group that voting to close the country school was the right thing to do.

He explained how kids attending the larger, consolidated school had higher test scores in reading, writing, and arithmetic compared to the country-school kids. Someone in the audience should have told him that there was more to an education than test scores. His research didn't turn up the fact that each of us, through eight years of Christmas programs, had learned how to stand up in front of an audience and say our piece. His research didn't show how upper-grade students helped lower-grade students with their lessons. He didn't mention how we, with different ethnic backgrounds and religions, had learned how to get along with each other. His research obviously didn't look into such things as how the country school gave rural communities an identity, and how the school provided a social center for the community.

He also said something that I never forgot. "I'm sorry to have to tell you folks, but your kids who have attended a one-room country school will likely grow up to be social misfits because they are so isolated from other people." He obviously didn't check on these "social misfits" who grew up to be successful farmers, lawyers, professors, doctors, and community leaders.

Lessons

- Reading, writing, arithmetic—and so much more.
- How to share and care for those who had less than I did.
- How to learn by myself and with others.

Chapter 5
High School Years

I began Wild Rose High School in the fall of 1947. I had just turned 14 and got to ride a school bus, one of two school buses that for the first time, were picking up farm kids attending Wild Rose High. The high school principal owned the buses and charged $1.25 a week for the ride. The bus ride was a long one, covering farm families living half way to Plainfield. The second bus brought in farm kids from east of Wild Rose. I was more than a little scared. I was accustomed to walking to school, which I had done for eight years when I attended Chain O'Lake School.

John Zubeck, who was a year ahead of me at Chain O' Lake, and was now a sophomore at Wild Rose High, met the big red, white, and blue bus when it arrived at the high school building. It was a big three-story building with a one-story gym attached to one side. John told me to follow him into the building, where he first showed me the restrooms, one for boys and one for girls. These were all new to me as neither the one-room school nor at home did we have indoor plumbing.

He then showed me the Freshman Home Room, as it was called. My fellow freshman students were already gathering there. This was also a new experience as I had been the sole member of my class during most of the years at the one-room country school. Now, I sat in a classroom with 19 other students, all freshmen at Wild Rose High School. There were four girls, none of whom I had previously known, and the rest were boys. The only boy I knew was Kenny Owens. Ken and I were members of the same 4-H club. His brother, Clayton Owens, was our 4-H leader.

I brought my own lunch and sat at my desk to eat it. Most of the other freshmen walked a couple of blocks to a place where lunch was served in the basement of one of the buildings on Main Street in Wild Rose. Lunch was 25 cents, if I remember. For my parents, however, that was another cost to be added to the school bus ride that they could scarcely afford. Thus I carried my lunch during my freshman year.

It was during the noon break that I first met Paul Wright, who was the baseball and basketball coach, as well as the math and history teacher, the director of the school plays, and in charge of the public speaking program. All the freshman boys were expected to try out for the baseball team, which was active in the fall as we had too few students to play competitive football. Because I was still recovering from polio, which I came down with when I was 13, I could barely walk and miserably failed my tryout for the team. This event only added to my feelings of worthlessness since I had come down with polio and couldn't do what other boys my age could easily do.

After the tryouts, Coach Wright took me aside. He saw how depressed I looked.

"How you doing?" he asked.

"Not well," I said, looking down at my feet.

"I'm sorry you didn't make the baseball team," he said, putting one of his big hands on my shoulder.

"So am I," I said, trying to hold back tears.

"I know about your polio challenge," he said.

I said nothing and continued looking at my feet.

"I have another idea for you," Coach Wright said.

I looked up at him, but didn't say anything.

"I think you should take the typewriting class," he said quietly.

"Typewriting is for girls," I said, wondering why he had come up with that strange suggestion.

"I think you would like it," he said. What he didn't tell me and he knew, was that the typewriting class was also the newspaper office for the high school newspaper, *The Rosebud*.

High School Years

Soon, I was not only learning how to type, but was also learning how to write news stories. By the time I was a senior, I was the editor of *The Rosebud*, and writing several of the articles, including an editorial for each monthly edition.

Paul Wright also got me into public speaking, something I had learned a bit about from my participation in the Christmas program at our country school. Mr. Wright had me announcing the basketball games in the fall, and participating in the public speaking program at the school and at the district level. I was enjoying both my writing experience and my speaking experience—skills I have used throughout my life.

I am forever thankful for Paul Wright and Bill Harvey (the typing teacher) for seeing something in me that I couldn't see in myself. Even though I was never able to participate in any sports, I still could do something interesting and useful for others.

As I attended my various classes, I discovered, that most of the subjects were of considerable interest to me. I liked Algebra and Geometry, which were challenging for several of my fellow students. I volunteered to help them with their struggles and decided that maybe I should be a teacher.

My 1951 high school graduation picture.

Lessons from 90 Years of Living

To my great surprise, my fellow students voted me class president when I was a sophomore and once more when I was a senior. And to my even greater surprise, when I was a senior, I learned that I was the valedictorian of my high school class. I liked to study—still do—but had no idea I was outranking my fellow students with my grades.

The other day, I found a copy of the valedictory talk I gave at my high school graduation. I was then 16 years old (May 1951).

Parents, fellow graduates, faculty, ladies and gentlemen. It is my rather sad duty as representative of my class, to bid farewell to our high school life. No graduating senior can fail to understand how we feel at this time. After four years of work, we have

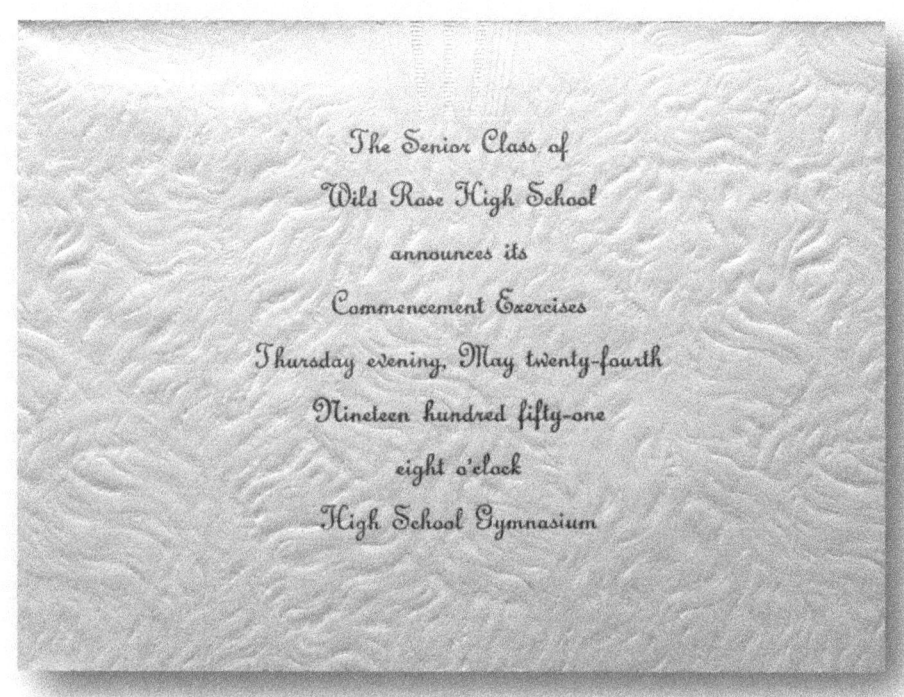

I graduated valedictorian of my high school class.
This enabled me to earn a scholarship to go to college.

reached our goal in high school. Tonight, the diplomas will be ours, the moment of success is at hand. We are reluctant to cast off the old ties and step out into the world on our own. We are glad and happy and yet deep down in our hearts there is a feeling of sadness. Tonight, many of our friends, whom we have known throughout our school life, will go their separate ways. We shall also miss deeply our teachers whom we are leaving behind. Anyone who has passed through a similar experience can understand how we feel.

Let us stop and think for a moment.

What about this world in which we are to spread our untried wings? What can it offer us? No one will deny that it is indeed in a sad state of affairs. No one will question the fact that a great part of the world is at war or preparing for war. We must admit that our future is somewhat uncertain. No doubt many of us will be a part of the armed services, perhaps located on the other side of the world. Others of us may be working in defense plants. The prospect of a third world war casts a black shadow over our future. With the world in such a condition as it is now, to what can a graduating senior look forward?

With these facts in mind, perhaps many of you would be interested in know how we feel about the future. In the first place, we have hope for the future. We are young and strong. We are armed with understanding, sympathy and tolerance. We know that beyond the dark clouds is a blue sky and a warm sun. We are not afraid to face the future.
 Secondly, we have faith. We have faith in the strength of our country and its ability to withstand attacks on our democratic ideals. We see this fact proved in previous attempts against our freedoms. We know what our country is and our desire is to keep it as nearly perfect as possible.
We have faith in God's justice and the final triumph of right will prevail.

Lessons from 90 Years of Living

We believe in the charter of the United Nations, and in the doctrine of peace and the brotherhood of men.

Finally, we are Americans. This is our country. It has given us what we have. It has made all of us what we are. We are willing to serve our country in whatever capacity it demands. We know the virtues of freedom, and we as Americans will do our best to keep our country the land of the free, and the home of the brave. For after the turmoil and shouting die, we know that there will be a place for us in the peace time ranks of our country, a place where we can work our destiny.

Lessons

- Accepting the advice of others who saw something in me that I didn't see in myself.
- How to write for publication in a typewriting class.
- How to help my fellow students with their math lessons.
- Discovering that I liked teaching and public speaking.

Part II
College Years

UW-Ag Hall, where I had my office.

CHAPTER 6
UNIVERSITY OF WISCONSIN—MADISON

In my spring and final semester of high school, I thought about whether or not I should plan to take up farming with Pa, which would have been the usual thing to do. I was the oldest son in the family and for generations of farm people, the oldest son usually took over the farming operation from his father. The problem was that I was still recovering from my bout with polio, which prevented me from walking without a limp, and caused me to tire earlier than I thought I should. I considered enrolling at Wisconsin State College, Stevens Point, in the conservation program they had. Stevens Point was close enough to the farm that I could come home most weekends to help with the farm work.

But then disaster struck the Herman Apps dairy herd of Holstein cattle. All the cattle, with the exception of one heifer that had been vaccinated, came down with brucellosis and had to be sold. Pa received a little indemnity money from the state for each animal sold, but not near enough to match our previous annual farm income from the dairy herd. There was no money for me to go to college. There was no money beyond the most basic necessities to keep the farm from going under.

Then a surprise. A few weeks before high school graduation, I learned that I was valedictorian of my senior class, which entitled me to a semester's free tuition at the University of Wisconsin in Madison. A semester's tuition at the time was $62.50. After a long discussion with both Pa and Ma, we agreed I should accept the tuition and enroll in the College of Agriculture at that "Big university in Madison," as Pa described it.

We looked into housing costs, and quickly decided I couldn't afford staying in a dormitory, where most freshmen stayed. With the help of my Uncle Wilbur, we found a single room in a rooming house on Orchard Street. Weekly cost—$5.00. The room even had a sink with hot and cold running water. At the time, we still did not have running water at our farm home. We bought an electric hot plate, and I was all set. I would be preparing most of my meals in my room, at considerably less cost than I would pay at a restaurant. The problem was—I knew next to nothing about cooking.

In mid-September, my mother, with Uncle Wilbur, drove me to Madison. I brought my typewriter that I had since high school days, two pairs of new khaki pants, two new dress shirts, and some new underwear. My mother had used some of her egg money to buy me these new clothes. "I want you to look nice," she said.

Pa did not come along to Madison, as he had to stay home to take care of chores—we had purchased a few milk cows to replace those lost to the dreaded brucellosis disease.

Ma and Uncle Wilbur dropped me off at my rooming house. I put my clothes away and sat down on my bed. I had never stayed overnight in a city. I had never been so alone. I knew no one in Madison. Would I like it here? I remembered how much I enjoyed the quiet of the country when I heard a siren, a sound I never heard at home. *Do I really belong here?* I wondered. *I am so much a country boy.*

One of the first classes I signed up for was Agronomy 1A. with Professor Henry Ahlgren, How interesting it was to learn about such farm crops as alfalfa beyond what I already knew. I knew how to make hay out of the crop but I didn't know there were several different varieties of alfalfa and that Professor Ahlgren had helped develop them.

Another first-semester class was Chemistry 1A, which had more students in the lecture section than were enrolled in the entire Wild Rose High School. Chemistry 1A proved impossibly difficult for me with its language of words I had never heard before.

The course not only offered three lectures a week, but also provided laboratories, and what were called "quiz sections," where smaller groups discussed what was presented in the labs and the lectures. Periodic quizzes were also offered. I received an F on my first quiz. In my 12 years of elementary and high school classes, I had never received an F grade. I went to see my academic advisor, Professor Ken Bucholtz. I told him I had gotten an F in Chemistry.

"It happens," he said.

"What am I going to do?" I asked. "Will I have to drop out of the university?"

Bucholtz laughed, "Of course not. The quiz grade doesn't even count toward your final grade," he said. "Tell you what I'm going to do. The Alpha Zeta honorary agriculture fraternity members offer consulting help to students like you. I'll find an AZ student to help you."

The AZ student met with me a couple times a week after the chemistry lecture. He went over my lecture notes with me, and helped me understand what I had heard in the lecture and what I had written down. I received a C at the end of the course, and a B after taking Chemistry 1B. I even came to like chemistry, once I understood its language.

Ironically, by the time I was a senior and a member of Alpha Zeta, I was helping freshman students with chemistry and other courses. Each time I did it, I saw myself four years earlier with the same struggles and concerns. I remembered how I had considered dropping out of the university after I had gotten the F—and realized how difficult it would have been for me to return home, after I had won a scholarship for being valedictorian of my high school class.

I graduated from the UW–Madison with honors.

LESSONS

- How to make a major life decision—attend college or not.
- Adjusting to the noises, and the hurry, hurry bustle of the city.
- Learning how to cook for myself.
- Learning how to take detailed notes from complicated lectures.
- Learning technical words I had never heard before.
- Learning how to deal with failure.
- Learning to accept help when offered.

CHAPTER 7
ROTC

Two years of ROTC (Reserve Officers Training Corps) courses were required for all the boys attending the University of Wisconsin in the fall of 1951, the year I enrolled. The draft was already taking hundreds of young men into military service, many of them serving in Korea. As long as I was in ROTC, I was draft deferred. I had a choice of either the Army or Air Force. I selected the Air Force ROTC. For some reason, I thought it would be fun to be a military jet pilot. After four years of Air Force ROTC, I could attend flight school and become a pilot.

When college began in the fall, I attended my first ROTC class, taught by a fulltime Air Force officer—in uniform. I began learning about the Air Force, which had come into existence as a separate organization of the military in 1947. Before that, it had been the Army Air Force. I also began learning about what it meant to be an Air Force Officer, which included some basic ideas about leadership. We were issued uniforms—they appeared to be left over from World War II. We were required to wear our uniforms when we attended ROTC classes.

I wasn't especially interested in the topics discussed, but two things remained important—I had a draft deferment, and upon completing four years of Air Force ROTC, I could attend flight school, and become a military pilot. That's what the literature said anyway.

I was most interested in my agricultural courses, and some basic courses such as botany, chemistry, entomology, and zoology. I discovered I really enjoyed these courses and what I was learning. Less so were my English courses. I got good grades in the basic science courses, once I had completed the remedial work, and lesser grades in English. I had hoped to polish my writing skills in the English courses, but I spent almost all of the time studying classic English literature, and not learning the craft of writing. I also realized that I'd better improve my ROTC grades or I wouldn't be accepted in advanced ROTC, which began in my junior year.

Upon completion of my sophomore year, I traveled to Truax Field (now Dane County Airport) where there was an Air Force base. I spent most of an afternoon being poked and probed by an Air Force doctor, who never once asked if I had had polio. As it turned out he was most interested in my eyesight. After several tests, which I failed, he said I could not continue in Air Force ROTC because my eyesight was not up to Air Force standards.

I was devastated with the news. Now I would be eligible for the draft and would likely end up fighting in Korea, as several of my high school classmates were already doing. And I would never become an Air Force pilot.

Back on campus one of my friends asked me how the exam had gone. "Not good," I answered. "Flunked the eye test. No advanced Air Force ROTC for me."

"So what are you gonna do?" my friend asked.

"I don't know," I answered. "I just don't know."

"Have you thought about applying for Army ROTC?"

"They probably wouldn't want me either," I said. I felt like crying.

"You should try it," he said. "I'm in Army ROTC, and my eyesight isn't all that good."

I thought of talking to my folks about my situation, but I thought better of. It would just give them one more thing to worry about. Neither of my parents had graduated from eighth grade. High school was a mystery to them. What went on at a university was even more of a mystery—especially ROTC. They did know it had provided me with a draft deferment—and I didn't want them to know that my draft deferment had disappeared.

ROTC

Following my friend's suggestion, I stopped by the Army ROTC office the next day. I explained that I had spent two years in Air Force ROTC and flunked the eye test so I couldn't go on in advanced Air Force ROTC. I indicated my interest in advanced Army ROTC, Transportation Corps. (With my bum leg, I figured I would probably get a ride while in the Transportation Corps.)

After another physical, where my eyesight met Army requirements, and a bit of paper work, I was in advanced Army ROTC. That fall, when I attended my first Transportation ROTC class, I noticed that several of my agriculture classmates were there. It felt good. I felt better as I buckled down to earn better-than-average grades in all of my classes, including Transportation Corps ROTC. I was working 40 hours a week (50 cents an hour) to earn enough money to eat and pay my rent. Most of the hours were accumulated in the evenings and on weekends. I also earned a small stipend from the Army for the two years I was in advanced ROTC.

The summer between my junior and senior year in college, I attended a six-week "ROTC summer camp." It was really six weeks of basic training to find out if we were cut out to be Army officers.

One early June morning in 1954, Dick Anderson, a ROTC friend, plus two other ROTC friends, and I started out for Fort Eustis, Virginia. We rode in Dick's car. At the time, I had only visited Illinois and Michigan, so this was an adventure for me from the very beginning. Our plan was to only stop for gasoline and restroom breaks, and keep driving the over 1000 miles from Madison, Wisconsin to Fort Eustis, Virginia. One person would drive for two hours, and the second one would read the map and keep the driver awake, and the third and fourth fellows would sleep. Then we would switch positions.

We drove through Chicago, along the lake front of Lake Michigan. No problems. Then we continued on until we got to the Pennsylvania Turnpike.

Lessons from 90 Years of Living

I later learned that it had opened on Oct 1, 1940. I'd never seen anything like it. Imagine two lanes of traffic going in both directions. Not too much later, we were in West Virginia, in rather mountainous country, which I had never experienced. I thought I knew what poverty was, but what I saw in West Virginia topped anything I had previously seen, and I had grown up during the Great Depression. I saw little kids, poorly dressed, standing outside log cabins. Farmers were working their fields with mules; I had no experience with mules.

Not long after that we were in the state of Virginia, and then we arrived at Fort Eustis. I was a bit travel weary and anxious about what would come next. I had earlier asked about what to expect from some of the ROTC seniors at the UW, who had attended the camp the previous summer. They would only smile, and say such things as, "You'll find out."

We were given work uniforms—fatigues, they were called, dark green in color—along with a heavy metal helmet with a lighter helmet liner, plus Army boots. Finally, we were given firearms—30 caliber M-1 carbines. I was assigned to a bunk in the bunkhouse, where a sergeant taught us how to make our beds. He said, "The top blanket should be so tight that when I toss a quarter on it, it will bounce."

We were shown where the mess hall was located, and the times for meals, and how some of us would likely have the opportunity to help with KP (kitchen patrol) duty. It was hardly an opportunity as it often meant cleaning out the grease trap in the kitchen and helping wash dishes. Physical training, including running a couple of miles each day, was early on our agenda. We did this every morning. Thankfully, farm work that I'd been doing after the semester at college ended, had gotten me in fairly good shape, including my polio leg, which sometimes hurt like the dickens after one of our many workouts.

The second week we were there, we were all loaded in the back of Army trucks and hauled to Camp A. P. Hill, located some distance north of Fort Eustis. There we would bivouac (camp outdoors in tents). This experience was to have us participate in a simulated combat situation, with active-duty soldiers as the enemy. We each had a backpack that contained half a pup tent, a blanket, a mess kit, and a folding shovel. Of course, we each had our carbines, but no ammunition.

The first thing we were instructed to do was to dig a foxhole near where we were to put up our pup tent. This was done with a little folding shovel. The hole was to be deep enough so your head would be below the surface of the ground when you bent down. It was heavy clay soil, as I remember, and not easy digging. Next, my tentmate and I broke out the two halves of our pup tent and buttoned them together, pounded in the tent pegs, set up the folding tent poles, and we were ready.

My tentmate was a college guy from New York City. He was more than a little anxious about what we were doing. He said he'd never slept in a tent, never been in such a dense woods, and never carried nor fired a rifle in his life. "It's going to be fine." I told him.

"But aren't there wild animals out here?" he asked.

"Probably," I answered, but they are likely more afraid of us than we are of them." I know he didn't believe me, as he crawled into our two-person pup tent and arranged his blanket on the floor of the tent.

The kitchen crew had set up a portable kitchen and with our mess kits and canteens in hand, we walked over to an opening in the woods where we would be eating supper. Tomorrow would be the battle—some three miles from where we were bivouacking. As a squad leader, I was an acting sergeant with twelve men under my command. I received a map and a compass, with the simulated combat area marked on the map.

Not long after supper, the sun began to set and we found our way to our tents. It soon was dark—very dark—as it was a cloudy night.

My tentmate was a pack of nerves. "It's so dark."

"Yes, it is," I said. "Good night for sleeping."

I almost immediately fell asleep, as I was tired from a long day, and knew the next day would even be more challenging as I led my squad into the mock battle. I was awakened by my tentmate sometime in the middle of the night. "Jerry, Jerry," he said nervously. "There is something crawling on our tent."

It had started to rain, and to my tentmate, the sound of raindrops on canvas sounded to him like some wild animal trying to get inside our tent and attack us.

"It's only rain," I said. "Go back to sleep." I listened for the rain for a few minutes, remembering how the rain sounded when it struck our barn roof. I fell back into a deep sleep, but before I did, I noticed that my tentmate was sitting by the tent opening holding his carbine. Good thing none of us had any ammunition.

The next morning, we dressed, and I assembled my squad of twelve men for a three-mile hike along a dusty trail to where the simulated battle was to take place. I had the map in one hand and the compass in the other. I didn't tell the officer who had made me acting sergeant in charge of a squad that a compass and map and I never got along very well. And on this day that proved true, as we walked for a mile or so we began hearing the loud "*kabooms*" of the heavy artillery the mock enemy was using to simulate what a soldier heard on a battlefield.

I called a halt for a bit of a rest as I studied my map and compass. We were soon on our way again, but in the wrong direction, as I later found out. My squad and I were an hour late getting to the battle. It was over. I saw some of my fellow ROTC candidates with splotches of what looked like white flour on the back of their uniforms. They were casualties of the mock battle. The officer in charge of the mock battle saw my squad and me and noticed that there were no casualties. We received a commendation for the good work we had done. I had my squad swear that they would not mention that we had not found the battle until it was over.

ROTC

The next day we were back at Fort Eustis, and on the firing range. We were learning how to use our M1 carbines. I didn't tell the sergeant in charge that I had been shooting a rifle since I was 12 years old, and that our farm family depended on wild meat for a goodly part of our diets. Most of my fellow ROTC members had never shot any kind of gun before, and a few were downright afraid to do it. Of course, now we were using live ammunition. (Unfortunately, no one in those days thought to use ear protection—one of the main reasons I have hearing loss now so many years later.)

I remember one of the guys was having trouble shooting his carbine. He turned around and pointed the weapon at the firing range sergeant without thinking what he was doing The sergeant's face turned white. He dropped to the ground and yelled to the guy with the carbine to turn around and not ever do that again.

Outside of the noise, I mostly enjoyed my time at the shooting range, as I was re-living some of my childhood. I must boast for a moment, I was quite a good shot with a .22 rifle. I was also a good shot with a .30 caliber carbine.

Another day, we traveled to Fort Story, Virginia, located near Virginia Beach, where we practiced laying land mines on the sandy ocean beach. I was never a fan of land mines. I still am not, as it is a gruesome device, killing and maiming both military and civilians.

The final activity, which proved the most challenging for the guys who had grown up in a big city with little opportunity to be in the great outdoors for any length of time, especially at night. It was called a night infiltration course. Live rounds of tracer 50-caliber machine gun bullets were fired over our heads as we crawled in the dark, through mud, obstacles, and barbed wire for 100 meters, almost the length of a football field. We each wore our combat boots and clothing and carried our combat backpack, as well as our .30 caliber carbine. Two things we were instructed not to do: 1) stand up because a machine gun bullet could cut you in two, and 2) above all keep your carbines dry and out of the mud. We were taught how to crawl, using our elbows and knees, to propel across the course that was marked with holes several feet deep.

When one of us got close to one of these holes, barely visible in the dark, our trainer would set off an explosive device that would create an ear-numbing noise and shoot a stream of water and mud several dozen feet into the air, falling on us as we crawled through the muck and mire. It didn't help that I had a bum knee left over from polio. On the other hand, because of my bad knee and leg, my upper body strength was better than most of the guys crawling through the course. Using my elbows and arms, I made my way through the challenging course and was one of the first to complete it—with no injuries and a mostly dry carbine.

Not everyone made it though the course—which meant they were washed out of ROTC. I never heard the number, but the event gave all of us a lot to talk about as we completed our six weeks of basic training, and returned to our homes.

Lessons

- When one door closes, look for another to open.
- No one can ever go it alone in life.
- How to compensate for a polio-injured leg.

Chapter 8
Summer Work and Campus Jobs

During the summers when I was attending college, from 1951 to 1955, I worked off the farm to earn enough money so I could continue to attend school, as my parents had no money to pay my tuition and other basic costs. (I had a scholarship for my first semester (fall of 1951).

Pickle Factory
The summer I reached age 18, (1952), I was hired by the H. J. Heinz Company to work as the manager of a cucumber salting station in Wild Rose. I had completed one year at the University of Wisconsin. I couldn't believe that I was a manager, but I did know a good deal about cucumbers, as we had a cucumber patch at the home farm for as long as I could remember. I recalled the many times I had visited the pickle factory, as every one called the place, since I was a little kid. During pickle season, we hauled our cucumbers to the pickle factory each day.

A photo of me during my years at the University of Wisconsin–Madison.

As manager, I supervised the work of five other people. Two men dumped cucumbers into the sorter, which separated them into five different sizes. One worked at the sorter to make sure there were no spoiled cucumbers. One took the sorted cucumbers and toted them to the wooden tanks where they would be dumped each evening before we could go home. One person was responsible for writing the checks and worked in our small office. For the four summers I managed the place, Monica Etheridge was the check writer.

In addition to supervising the crew, I was responsible for weighing the cucumbers in each grade. Farmers who brought in cucumbers were paid based on the weight of each grade they brought in. About 10:00 each evening, farmers were done delivering cucumbers for that day. The work for the pickle factory staff was just beginning, as we now had to dump these many hundreds of pounds of cucumbers into each of five wooden tanks according to their sizes.

The smallest cucumber was a number one. The largest was a number five. I kept a record of how many pounds of cucumbers we dumped into each tank each day. I turned this information into Monica, and her task, besides writing checks, was figuring out the salt and water to be put in each silo each day, based on the weight of the cucumbers added to the tank. She followed a formula from H. J. Heinz.

Once the cucumbers were in a silo, we added the appropriate amount of salt and water. Each morning, I measured the salt level in each silo with a salinity meter and sent that information, along with a record of pounds of cucumbers received, as well as pounds of salt and gallons of water added to each tank to the Heinz Company in Pittsburgh. Sometimes it was two in the morning before the day's work was completed and we could go home. We worked six days a week, from late July to early September. Sundays and rainy days we had off. Both Monica and I received $1.25 an hour; the rest of the crew received $1.00 an hour. I managed the pickle station during the summers of 1952 to 1955.

Pea Viner Manager

In the early summers of 1952 and 1953, I managed a crew working on a field pea viner located north of Markesan, Wisconsin. I earned $1.25 an hour. The crew I managed each earned $1.00 an hour. The general pea harvest ran from mid-June to late July, ahead of the cucumber harvest.

A pea viner is a large machine that separates peas from their vines and pods. The machine was powered by a Farmall M tractor engine. One of my jobs was to keep the engine running from 8:00 a.m. to 2:00 a.m. the following morning. Farmers hauled their pea vines to the viner, and dumped them on a little platform in front of the machine.

Two workers pitched the pea vines into the vining machine, a miserable, back-breaking job, as the vines were often tangled around each other. A third man worked on the pea stack, receiving spent vines and pods, and forking them onto a pile, which grew ever taller as the pea harvesting season continued. A fourth worker filled wooden boxes with peas, which I weighed before they were stacked in a shady place by the viner. A truck stopped by every two hours or so to haul the peas to the canning factory in Markesan. I weighed each box of peas, and recorded the numbers for each load of peas delivered to the viner.

My duties, in addition to weighing the peas, maintaining records, and keeping the engine and the viner operating, included repairing broken chains and drive belts, and lubricating the machine each morning before we began work. My biggest challenge was managing the men, some of whom were not good workers. Granted, the work was hard, the hours long, and the temperature 80 degrees or more each day.

The crew was an interesting mixture of ages and work ethics. One was a college student, like me, and believed he was above all the other workers. I didn't tell him that I was also a college student. For him, I was just a farm boy. Another worker was a high school teacher, trying to earn a little extra money and was a good worker. An older man, in his 60s, was a hard worker, but I soon discovered was a heavy drinker. A young Black man, a Jamaican, in his early twenties, worked hard, never complained about anything, and seemed to enjoy work at the viner. Another farm boy rounded out the crew. He also worked hard, never complained, and was disliked by the college boy because the farm boy worked too hard.

The older man, who was usually drunk by noon, was my first major concern. I gave him the task of working the pea stack as I didn't want him to get caught in the viner's many moving parts. I talked to the fellow, and each time I talked to him, he said he would quit drinking. But he didn't. I figured out that he must be hiding his bottle of booze somewhere around the pea viner. One day, I shut down the viner, and instructed the viner workers to help me look for his bottle, which they all did.

I finally found it, tucked into a corner of the viner stack. Everyone gathered around me, wondering what I was going to do next. The owner of the bottle stood right in front of me. I don't know why I chose this action. But I did. I opened the bottle, held it up high and poured out the contents of the bottle while everyone watched. No one could see that I was shaking in my boots, anticipating that the bottle's owner would take a swing at me. But he didn't.

"Ok, everyone back to work," I said as I started the machine once more. I breathed a sigh of relief. For the rest of the season everyone worked hard, including the fellow who once was drunk by noon each day. I knew his family needed the money he earned, so I gave him a second chance.

Campus Jobs

Window washing, shoe polishing, taking in boat piers. Painting fire escapes. I did them all. I knew I had to work to earn enough money for food and to pay my rent in a private home—$5.00 a week.

School of Music

For my last two years as a student at the university, I worked for more than 40 hours a week at a job in the University of Wisconsin School of Music. Unfortunately, the pay was only 50 cents an hour. Generally, I worked from 6 p.m. to 10 p.m. from Monday to Friday, and from 9 a.m. to 10 p.m. on Saturday and Sunday.

My job was to manage music students practicing in the School of Music practice building, which had been an apartment house located across Park Street from the main School of Music building. My job was to assign music students to various practice rooms. Each student had access to the room for an hour. I had a little office located under the stairway to the second floor. Each hour, one of my jobs was to walk past each practice room, stop, listen and smell. I was to smell for smoke—no smoking allowed. I was to check that the student was practicing music, and not practicing some hanky-panky with a boyfriend or girlfriend. I described this part of my job as checking for smoking and smooching, and the prevention there of. When one or both pieces of rule-breaking was occurring, I quietly knocked on the door, and if I saw what I suspected, I said, "Stop that or I will have to report you to the dean."

In the two years that I worked there, I never once reported anyone to the dean. No one wanted to be reported and lose access to a practice room. The practice rooms were not insulated, so the mixture of piano, violin, drum, trumpet and more virtually shook the building when every room was occupied, which was most of the time. In between tours around the building, every hour, I could study. I learned to block out all the background noise.

About once a month, it was my job to arrange the big room in Music Hall for a concert, determining where the violins were to be, the trumpets, the clarinets, etc. When I first began working there, I didn't know a bassoon from a piccolo. A music professor patiently showed me how to arrange things.

LESSONS

- Learning the difference between being a manager, and being an hourly worker.
- Learning how to manage a crew of various ages, backgrounds, and work experience.
- Learning how to study in the midst of loud noise all around me.
- Learning how to earn enough money to stay in college and receive my bachelor's degree in four years..

PART III
POST-COLLEGE YEARS

My first full-time job was as a university Extension Agent in Green Lake County. I lived in this trailer.

CHAPTER 9
FIRST JOB AFTER COLLEGE

In June 1955, I was commissioned as a second lieutenant in the US Army as part of the graduation ceremony from UW–Madison. I was to serve two years of active duty and four more years as a reservist. My orders were to serve in Germany for two years, beginning in January of 1956. The Korean War had ended in 1953.

My brother Donald graduated from Wild Rose High School that year and was waiting to go to barber school in January of 1956. I couldn't get a regular job because no one would hire me for six months. So I looked for more seasonal work besides my job managing the pickle factory in Wild Rose from July to September.

Donald and I heard they were hiring workers at a cranberry marsh near Wisconsin Rapids—the pay was good ($1.00 an hour). The three of us—Donald, neighbor boys Jim and Dave Kolka, and I applied. We looked forward to working outside, and besides this was something we hadn't done before.

Wisconsin's history with cranberries goes back a long, long way. Cranberries are native to Wisconsin. They were well known to the Native Americans long before the first Europeans arrived in the state. They grew abundantly in marshy areas, especially in central Wisconsin counties. Native Americans ate cranberries fresh; they ground them and mixed them with cornmeal and baked the mixture into bread. They dried cranberries with wild game to make pemmican. Sometimes they mixed cranberries with maple sugar to soften the berries tart taste. Native Americans also knew about cranberries' medicinal qualities believing that they calmed nerves. They also were used as poultices to draw poison from wounds. These early people in Wisconsin used cranberry juice to dye blankets and rugs as well.

What is the source of the name for this tart, native berry? It is believed that the early Dutch or German settlers called the fruit "craneberries" because the cranberry stem and blossom resembled the neck, head and beak of the sandhill crane. Early settlers in Wisconsin, who lived within easy traveling distance of a wild cranberry bog, picked cranberries for their own use long before anyone grew them commercially. Edward Sacket of New York is credited with starting the first commercial cranberry operation in Wisconsin. Around 1860 he purchased seven hundred acres of bog land covered with cranberry vines north of Berlin in Waushara County. By 1865 he was producing more than 900 barrels a year of cranberries that sold for $15 dollars a barrel. Soon other cranberry growers joined Sacket and Waushara County experienced a bit of a cranberry boom.

In addition to Waushara County, wild cranberries also grew in Jackson, Juneau, Monroe, and Wood counties. In 1871, the first cultivated cranberries in the Wisconsin River Valley were planted near present-day Cranmoor in Wood County. By1895, the center of commercial cranberry growing had shifted to Wood County, to where my brother and I harvested cranberries. Starting in 1994, Wisconsin led the nation in cranberry production out pacing long-time leader, Massachusetts. At this writing, Wisconsin continues to be the leading producer of cranberries in the nation.

In 1955, the cranberry industry was just beginning to shift from hand-harvesting (which we did) to mechanical harvesting (which is done now). For hand-harvesting, we each received a cranberry rake, which is a little wooden box with an open end with tines on it and two bow handles, and a pair of hip boots. The cranberry bog was flooded so that the ripe, red cranberries floated and thus could be more easily gathered with our rakes. The water was knee deep, sometimes a little more, and on chilly October mornings was cold, cold, cold.

In addition to the rake and the hip boots, we each pulled behind us a floating wooden box, which was tied to our belts with a short rope. When our rake was full, we dumped the cranberries in the box. And when the bushel box was full, we carried it to the high ground that surrounded each bog. But before we got to the high ground we carefully navigated a narrow wooden plank placed across a water filled ditch. One misstep and we were in water up to our arm pits. One inaccurate swing with the rake, and a tine would puncture a hip boot and we'd have a wet foot all day. My hip boots had patches upon patches by the end of the season.

We worked in a long line, about eight or ten of us, with the person on the far right setting the pace—we had to keep up with that person, and often times, our arms felt like they'd come out of their sockets. On my first day, I snagged one of the tines with my rake on one of my hip boots, tearing a hole in it. I had a wet, cold foot and leg the rest of the day. That night, I patched the hole and it was onward the next day. Most of the rakers were high school kids from the area, and after a week of wet feet, I was not the only one who snagged his boots and had a sore back. I heard a goodly amount of grumbling. Because I was a bit older, several of the high school kids asked me if we could do something about the poor working conditions. I suggested we could strike. And that's what we did. After the lunch break one day, we continued to sit on the bank of the bog. The foreman, a rather mean-spirited chap, said in a loud voice, "Time to get back to work." None of us moved.

"We are on strike," I said.

"You can't do that," he said.

"But we did." I said, now wondering if this was the wise thing to do.

The foreman was soon on his two-way radio that he carried with him at all times, and a half hour later, the owner of the cranberry bog, an older woman, appeared. She was a gray-haired, soft-spoken, and as we learned, a very smart lady.

She parked her pickup and walked over to where we were sitting on the bank of the bog. I expected the worst, and wondered what I had gotten my fellow workers into.

"Nice day. How's it going, boys?"

"Not so good," I said, quietly.

"What seems to be the problem?" she asked.

"The bog's plenty weedy," I said. "We should be getting more than $1.00 an hour to rake these cranberries." There, I'd said it. *What would happen next?*

For a couple minutes, we all sat quietly. George, the foreman, sat off to the side, not saying anything, but listening intently and smirking a bit. Did he know something we didn't know?

Then the owner lady said, "You're right. This bog is weedier than it ought to be. Tell you what. How would it be if I gave each of you a little something more for each box you rake each day beyond a base amount, to make up for the difficult raking? I'll talk with George to see the average number of boxes you rake now, and that will be the base. After you reach the base amount, you'll get the bonus for each box you rake."

I looked at my fellow workers, "What to do you think, boys? Hold up your hand if you like the idea."

Every hand went up except one. He was an older guy who worked at the head of line of us workers and set the pace for how fast or slow we raked.

At day's end, I knew we had been snookered. Not only did we lose a few hours of pay when we were striking, we were now working faster so we would get a little extra money for our work and the boss lady got her bog raked faster.

LESSONS

- How to work cooperatively with other laborers.
- Think through some anticipated action before attempting it.

CHAPTER 10
ARMY ACTIVE AND RESERVE DUTY

I looked forward to serving two years active duty in the Army Transportation Corps followed by a minimum of six years as a reserve officer. In the fall of 1955, I was helping out on the home farm, managing the pickle factory, which I had done the previous three summers, and working in the cranberry harvest before going on active duty in January of 1956. Here is a little of what the Transportation Corps mission is:

> *The U.S. Army Transportation Corps' mission is to move troops, equipment, and supplies around the world to support the National Military Strategy. The Transportation Corps is a combat service support branch that was established in July 1942. They use trucks, boats, and planes to transport personnel and material by land, air, sea, and rail. The Transportation Corps trains soldiers and civilians, and develops concepts and doctrine for transportation services."* [Source: www.transportation.army.mil.]

One day in November 1955, George Collum, the depot agent in Wild Rose, called. I never got a phone call in those days, especially from the depot agent. "Jerry," George said. "Could you come down to the depot? I've just gotten a telegraph from the Army for you. I can't make heads or tails of it." After my graduation from the University of Wisconsin in 1955, I had received orders to travel to Germany, where I would spend two years on active duty. I drove down to the depot with Pa's car—I had sold my 1949 Ford to my brother Donald. I also sold most of civilian clothes in preparation for wearing an army uniform for two years.

George and I read the telegraph together. The gist of it was that my orders had been changed. I would not be going to Germany for two years, but would serve six months of active duty at Fort Eustis, Virginia, where I had done my basic training the previous summer, and then serve a minimum of six years in the Army Reserve.

On an early January day in 1956, my lieutenant friend Dick Anderson, who had a change in orders as well, and I, drove from Wisconsin to Fort Eustis, Virginia. Arriving there, we were assigned to housing in the bachelor officer quarters at the base, which was the center for the Army's Transportation Corps. These quarters were a considerable upgrade from where we stayed when we were in basic training a previous summer.

Wearing our uniforms, with the single gold bar denoting 2nd Lieutenant, we were saluted by everyone who had a rank below ours. And we had to salute back. This was something I had to get used to. Of course, we had to salute everyone who had a rank above us as well, including first lieutenants who wore a single silver bar to denote their rank.

On Monday morning, a room full of new 2nd lieutenants reported to a large room where we were introduced to 1st Lieutenant Half, who would be in charge of us now. We would spend the first three months of active duty attending the Transportation Officers Basic Course. It was here that we would learn in-depth what the Transportation Corps was all about and be introduced to where we might spend the following three months of our active duty time.

In some ways, it was like being back in college again, although we spent most of our time out of the classroom, doing hands-on learning. We first learned about the cargo ships that were a part of the Corps. I spent several days working as a stevedore, loading and unloading large boxes of I knew not what, into the cargo hold of a ship. It was hard work, not too different from stacking hay bales in a haymow back on the home farm.

Next, as I recall, I was becoming acquainted with airplanes designed to carry both personnel as well as their equipment. We practiced loading and unloading them. Then we became acquainted with both 2½ ton trucks as well as semi-trucks. We each got to drive both kinds of trucks. My farm background proved useful. I discovered that the semi-truck's transmission was exactly the same as the one on our Farmall H tractor. I had no trouble driving it, except it was several times longer even when the Farmall was hitched to a hay wagon.

We then became familiar with the DUKW, a 2½ ton truck that was converted into a vehicle that would operate in water as well on land. It was one of the fun things to learn about and to drive. It was commonly known as a DUCK.

We also learned about movement control strategies, which were used to decide which form of transportation should be used for a given situation. There were no computers available in 1956, so we were doing all the juggling and judging as to which transportation approach to use.

In the evenings, my fellow officers and I gathered at the officer's club at Fort Eustis. I learned about my fellow officers, where they grew up and what that was like. Such places as Detroit, Philadelphia, New York, and other smaller cities were represented. I believe I was the only one who had grown up on a farm. At the time, I was working on acting like a city person, leaving my farm background behind me. I soon discovered, that my fellow officers who pushed me to share some of my rural upbringing, said that it was pretty darn interesting. I began to think, maybe I should spend my work career taking advantage of my farm background..

The time at TOBAC, as we called the Transportation Officer Basic Course, flew by and we were each assigned to a working transportation unit for our remaining three months of active duty.

I was assigned to a Movement Control unit. Its home was at Fort Eustis, so I didn't have to move to another army base.

My main activity during my three months as a Movement Control Officer was to plan the loading of cargo ships that would resupply the Distance Early Warning (DEW line) radar stations located in northern Canada. "The DEW Line was the northernmost and most capable of three radar lines in Canada and Alaska. The first of these was the joint Canadian-United States Pinetree Line, which ran from Newfoundland to Vancouver Island just north of the Canada–United States border . . ." [Source: List of DEW Line Sites] .The cargo ships were headed for Hudson Bay in Canada, where it was free of ice during late summer months and early autumn.

I was just settling in to my new active duty work, when it was over and I was on my way back home, and prepared to serve the rest of my six years of Army time as a reserve officer. I was assigned to the Fourteen Corps with headquarters in Minneapolis. I learned I should join a local reserve unit, when I would attend weekend meetings, along with two weeks of active duty at a summer camp.

Upon arriving back at the Wild Rose home farm in July, I took some time off from farm work to drive to Madison, where I met with my undergraduate advisor, Walter Bjoraker. I told him I had changed my mind about teaching high school agriculture, and wondered about enrolling in a graduate degree program to earn a master's degree. He said the department had recently hired a new assistant professor, George Sledge, and he had assigned to him a graduate student, half/time research assistantship—and would I like to have it? I quickly said, "Yes" That would help solve my money problems.

I informed my contact person at the 14th Corps what my plans were for the 1956 academic year, and asked that I be excused from joining a local reserve unit. He said "Yes" to my suggestion, but said that I should enroll in the Transportation Corps Correspondence School to take the place of belonging to a

I spent ten years on active and reserve duty for the US Army.

reserve unit. In addition to the correspondence school work, I agreed to attend two-week summer camps each year of my reserve duty.

I continued as a student of the TC Correspondence School until I left the reserves in 1965. I attended several two-week summer camps, each interesting in its own way. The first one I attended was during the summer of 1958. I was excused from attending summer camp in 1957, as I was completing my graduate degree and beginning work as an Extension Agent in Green Lake County, Wisconsin. Fourteenth Corps assigned me to a group that was to attend summer camp at Camp McCoy, which was near Sparta, Wisconsin.

When I arrived at Camp McCoy on a Sunday evening, I met the officer in charge, who said he didn't know what to do with me, this 2nd Lieutenant. He soon learned that a captain also was attached to the unit for the two weeks. He decided to have the captain and me evaluate his unit's summer camp activity. I first needed to get a military driving license, which I did. Then I checked out a Jeep from the motor pool, and for two weeks, the captain and I prowled the roads and trails of Camp McCoy, making a few notes here and there, and enjoying the many interesting acres of the camp.

A second memorable camp was LeRoy Johnson, near New Orleans. Again I was assigned to a unit, but this time I had various responsibilities, such as supervising the time the men were on a firing range. I was a 1st Lieutenant at the time. Several days of the two weeks we spent at a camp near Biloxi, Mississippi on the Gulf of Mexico The men were practicing loading and unloading DUCKs from a cargo ship anchored a half mile or so from shore As I recall, the boxes we unloaded and then loaded again were filled with sawdust.

It was a windy day, and more than one DUCK, approaching the cargo ship with its load of sawdust boxes slammed into the ship, knocking off some paint. This resulted in loud shouting from someone on the ship. Each DUCK's trip from the ship to shore resulted in a goodly amount of sea water splashing into the DUCK. Upon arriving on shore, the driver needed to open a bilge cover allowing the sea water to drain before once more taking a load of sawdust to the ship. One driver forgot to replace the bilge cover, drove out to the ship, and saw his DUCK sink. No lives were lost and considerable quiet laughter took place. I don't recall how the sunken DUCK was retrieved from the bottom of the Gulf.

A third two-week summer camp was also notable. I was still a 1st lieutenant, waiting to be promoted to captain. I was assigned to a diesel locomotive repair shop at Fort Eustis, Virginia. The regular officer in charge was on two-week summer leave. The master sergeant in charge of the repair shop shook my hand when I reported for duty, and asked if I knew diesel locomotive repair. "I know absolutely nothing about diesel locomotive repair," I truthfully answered.

"Tell you what," the sergeant said, "If you can get me out of the dreaded Saturday parades, I'll write a positive report for you," he said.

"Deal," I said, as he shook my hand again.

I got him out of the parades, which I didn't mind doing. And he gave me a positive report.

Along the way, as I continued doing correspondence study, I was promoted to captain, with a promise I would soon make major. In 1965, after completing ten years of active and reserve duty, my wife Ruth, busy looking after our three little kids, asked if maybe I could resign from all this "army stuff." I didn't argue with her. The memories remain, most of them positive.

Lessons

- I learned who I was, and what I was able to do.
- Military rules could be flexible, if a reasonable reason for asking them was offered.
- Active and reserve military duty considerably broadened my view of the world.

> Mr. and Mrs. Herman Apps and Darrel Apps of Black River Falls drove to Green Bay last Tuesday evening where they attended a farewell banquet for Jerold Apps. Jerold has been 4-H club agent for Brown Co. for 2½ years. He and his family moved to Madison Thursday, where he will be assistant state 4-H leader.

This clipping announced my move to Madison and my next job.

CHAPTER 11
UNIVERSITY OF WISCONSIN WORK

I worked for the College of Agricultural and Life Sciences at the University of Wisconsin–Madison for 38 years, beginning in 1957 when I was hired as an Extension Agent for Green Lake County. My work week was to be Monday to Saturday. I had just finished a master's degree in Agricultural Education. On my first day of work—Saturday, June 15, 1957—I arrived at the Green Lake County Court House, at 8:00 a.m. There I met Willie Gjermandson, the Extension Office Chair, who was surrounded by several people.

"Welcome to Green Lake County," Willie said, shaking my hand. We had met a few weeks earlier when I was hired. "These are 4-H leaders who want to meet you." Willy introduced me to several men and women. "We are all traveling to Patrick Lake's 4-H Camp, over in Adams County." He pointed to the west. "It's our annual clean-up day before the camping season starts. Our 4-H members spend two week camping there each year. One week for older 4-H members, one week for younger ones."

On our drive over to Patrick's Lake, Willie explained that the camp had once been a Civilian Conservation Corps camp, and was a bit rustic back in the 1930s. "It has electricity, but no indoor plumbing." Just like at home I thought as we continued our drive. When we arrived at the camp, which included a kitchen-dining hall, two bunkhouses, and two outhouses on the shore of an attractive 30-acre lake.

Willie proceeded to list the tasks that needed doing: sweeping and cleaning the bunkhouses. scrubbing the kitchen and dining hall, raking the camp grounds, and digging new holes for the outhouses. Hands went up for the various tasks, except no hands went up for digging the outhouse holes. I held up my hand. Several people remembered that I had a master's degree and now was volunteering to dig outhouse holes. None of them realized that I had done the job several times before on the home farm, and knew how to do it.

After five years working as an Extension Agent in Green Lake, and then Brown County, from 1960 to 1962, I was hired as publications editor for the state 4-H office, which was part of the College of Agriculture on the UW–Madison campus. One day, in the spring of 1964, Walter Bjoraker, the chair of the Department of Agricultural and Extension Education came into my office. Walt had been my major professor for both my BS and MS degrees.

"Jerry, I've got a problem," he began. I had no idea where this discussion was going, but I had lots of respect for Walt and listened carefully.

"As you know, Professor Duncan is teaching in Brazil this coming year, and I need someone to teach his course. Would you be interested?"

For a minute or so, I couldn't think how to answer. I had taken the course myself a few years ago, so I knew the content. But was I prepared to be a college professor?

"I'll be happy to give it a try," I said.

Professor Duncan decided to stay abroad a second year and Walt asked me if I would be interested in working full-time in the department, leaving behind my editorial work in the 4-H office. I agreed to do it, but there was a major snag. I didn't have a Ph.D. degree, and all new hires in the college must have a Ph.D. degree. Walt said he had arranged a meeting for me with Dean Pound to discuss my situation.

"I've thought about Walt hiring you and here's what I've decided," the dean said.

I wouldn't have been surprised if he told me that he couldn't approve of the hire because I didn't have a Ph.D. degree, but that's not what he said. "Tell you what, we'll hire you, but before we can promote you from assistant professor to associate professor, and before we can give you a raise in salary, you must complete a Ph.D. degree."

I had never thought about working on a Ph.D. degree, as I knew it required at least three more years of graduate work. I could work and study part-time for three years, and then I must take off from teaching one year to work on my research and write my Ph.D. dissertation.

"And I must add," the dean said. "You must do your Ph.D. outside the department where you are teaching."

All I could think to say was, "I'll have to talk this over with Ruth, my wife." We had three little kids at the time, and we were poor as church mice. But she agreed, and I completed a Ph.D. with a major in Adult Education and minor in Rural Sociology. Those were a tough three years, for me, for Ruth and for our three little kids. The dean kept his promise.

When I graduated with a Ph.D. degree, he saw that I got promoted to associate professor and I received an increase in salary. I taught for 30 years in the College of Agriculture and Life Sciences, including seven years as department chair. See my book, *Once a Professor: A Memoir of Teaching in Turbulent Times*. (Wisconsin Historical Society Press. 2018), for stories about my college teaching.

LESSONS

- Sometimes it is necessary in one's life, to move back a bit, so one can move forward to a higher level opportunity.

Part IV
Early Retirement Years

My first book, *The Land Still Lives,* was published in 1970.

CHAPTER 12
FULL-TIME WRITER, PART-TIME TEACHER

When I was 60 years old, I retired from my position as professor at the UW–Madison so I could write full-time, something I always wanted to do, and something I am now doing.

I began writing columns as part of my work in 1957, when I wrote a weekly column for the *Berlin Journal* in Berlin, Wisconsin. At the time, I was working as an Extension Agent for the UW's College of Agriculture. In 1960, I moved to Green Bay and worked there as an Extension Agent, writing columns for the *Green Bay Press Gazette*. Ray Pagel was Farm Director for the paper at the time. He would have made a good English teacher, for with a red pen, he took my columns apart and showed me how to make them better. He showed me how to say something with 500 words or less. For his patience and instruction, I am forever grateful.

In 1962, my wife Ruth, three-month-old baby daughter Susan, and I moved to Madison where I became Publications Editor for the State 4-H Department, which was a part of the College of Agriculture. I edited the many 4-H bulletins that went out by the thousands to 4-H members around the state. The bulletins ranged from how to raise a dairy calf to tips for sewing and canning. I had no time for column writing, indeed no time for any of my own writing. However, I did do a fair amount of rewriting of other people's work.

In 1964, I began teaching in the Department of Agricultural and Extension Education in UW–Madison's College of Agriculture. I was learning a new job, and helping take care of my family, which left little time for column writing or any creative writing.

In 1966, while on leave from my teaching to work on completing my doctorate, Ruth and I enrolled in an evening creative writing course, taught by Al Nelson. Now for the first time, I was learning about freelance writing including how to pick a topic, how to select a possible publisher, how to write a query letter and more. (A query letter is a letter to a potential publisher to see if they would be interested in my work).

During the workshop, Ruth wrote an article with recipes for preparing venison. She mailed it to *Outdoor Life Magazine*. She sent no query letter, just the article. Almost by return mail, she received a check for $50.00. Her comment to me, "Nothing complicated about this freelance writing business." I suggested she write some more articles. "I may get around to it," she said. "Seems a bit too easy to do." She was kidding with me, of course.

Meanwhile, I began sending query letters and articles to an assortment of magazines—*Reader's Digest*, *The Atlantic Monthly,* and others. Each time, my article came back with a rejection letter. In 1966, thinking back to my experience writing columns when I was an Extension Agent, I decided to contact the *Waushara Argus*, the weekly newspaper I had grown up with, to see if they might publish a weekly column of mine.

Howard Sanstadt was the editor at the time, and he agreed to publish a few columns to see what kind of reaction he got from *Argus* readers. The reaction was positive. For ten years, I wrote weekly columns for the *Argus*, 520 of them. In addition, I began writing columns for the Hortonville and the New London weekly papers, along with the *Central Wisconsin Resorter*—all of which were owned by Mr. Sandstadt. Payment was $5.00 a column.

A bit later, I wrote weekly columns for the *Country Today* and *Agriview* newspapers. In recent years, I wrote a column for the *Wisconsin State Farmer*. I also wrote a weekly column for 15 years as both a blog and an entry on my Facebook Page. In 2023, I wrote my last column—something I had done for 60 years,

Also in 1966, Robert Gard, who became my writing mentor, suggested I enroll in the Rhinelander School of Arts, which was a two-week summer writing workshop. Bob suggested I take August Derleth's fiction writing workshop, which I did. Derleth, a well-known Wisconsin writer, had penned several Wisconsin-based novels along with several nonfiction books.

After finishing the workshop, I said to Ruth, "I can do that. I can write a novel." And I did—I published eight novels for adults and three for young readers. In 1971, my first nonfiction book, *The Land Still Lives*, was published by Wisconsin House, a small publishing company started by Robert Gard. Bob was also a UW–Madison professor.

Keeping a Journal

I have been writing in a journal since 1966, almost every day, but always several times a week. I write about the weather, I write about what is happening in my life. I write about some problem I am facing. I include information about my friends—as several of my friends have recently passed I put their obituaries in my journal.

Teaching Writing Workshops.

I began teaching writing workshops at the School of the Arts in Rhinelander in 1971. I taught writing workshops for 42 years—30 plus years at Rhinelander and another 30 at The Clearing in Door County. Several years I taught at both places. Here is what I wrote, after two of the workshops I taught at the Clearing—one a week-long workshop, and the second a day-long workshop.

> *I spent a delightful week teaching a writing workshop at The Clearing in Door County. People attended from Iowa, Minnesota, Illinois, and Wisconsin, all interested in turning their memories into memoirs. Seventeen writers gathered each morning to write stories from such prompts as: "I wish someone had told me . . ." and "Ten things that annoy me. .*

." They drew house plans for homes where they grew up, triggering memories of smells, sights, and sounds. They listened to country music that told a story. They wrote about people who made a difference in their lives and turning points that sent them in new directions. They discussed journaling and how to do research for their stories. They laughed; they hugged, and sometimes, there were tears, as not all memories are pleasant ones. But at week's end, in the midst of the hottest and most humid seven days that Door County remembered in some time, they wrote their stories—wonderful stories that came from the heart.

Last Saturday was a beautiful fall day at The Clearing in Door County where thirty of us gathered for my annual one-day writing workshop that I call "Writing From Your Life." Plenty of fall color. The waters of Green Bay were deep slate; the birch still showed some yellow and the sky was clear and blue.

The writers gathered to share stories—stories of early memories, of first toys, of growing up, of first jobs for pay, of joyous moments and many not as joyous as a few tears fell. These writers of several generations filled pages with tales from their lives—stories long forgotten, by some at least. They shared their tales with each other and laughed and nodded knowingly, for though the details may have been different, the stories of each generation had many similarities as well.

LESSON LEARNED

- From my writing students, I learned much, about life and living, and about writing.

CHAPTER 13
THE POWER OF STORYTELLING

A few years ago, I was part of a storytelling workshop held in New York City. As the leader of the workshop, I had the opportunity to speak to United Nations delegates at the UN building about the importance of stories in the lives of people. When I finished my comments, several African delegates walked up to the stage to speak with me.

One woman said, "We know the importance of stories in our culture and in our country."

I replied that I was well aware of that, for I had long known about countries where storytelling is embedded in their culture. But then she said something I've never forgotten. With a quiet voice, she said, "In your country, you have allowed others to tell your stories for you." She was referring to movies and television.

I have been telling stories since I was a kid. I grew up hearing them. Pa was a first-rate storyteller, so were several of our farm neighbors. When the neighbors gathered for threshing, silo-filling, corn-shredding and wood-sawing, they told stories. They exchanged stories during and after the shared meals. They told stories during the breaks in work. Driving by a field of Amish shocked oats or shocked corn today triggers memories of stories from my growing-up years on a farm.

As a kid, I listened to radio programs: *The Lone Ranger, Terry and the Pirates, Captain Midnight, Jack Armstrong*, and others. The stories tapped into my imagination. I lived the stories right along with the radio actors who were telling them. I saw the pictures in my mind as clearly as if they were printed on paper.

Whether the story was told by John Steinbeck, Ernest Hemingway, or the neighbor who lived down the road, they were all important to me. When I was growing up, storytelling was an integral part of our rural community, especially stories with a humorous twist. Whenever a couple or more farmers got together, whether it was at the grist mill waiting for their cow feed to be ground, or over the back fence when two neighboring farmers stopped their work for a chat, storytelling almost always resulted.

Storytelling was not only a way for people to socialize, it also offered the storytellers and their listeners the opportunity to share something about themselves that was difficult to share in any other way. With stories, farmers shared their innermost thoughts, feelings, and emotions—something no farmer wanted to or perhaps didn't know how to talk about. Storytellers also revealed something of their personal uniqueness. Each storyteller had his or her own style of stringing words together in such a way that they evoked a response from the listener, or the reader, if the story was written.

Most rural storytellers stayed close to the facts, but they did embellish here and there, as time passed and the story was repeated. This was especially so for stories involving fishing and hunting. Beyond fishing and hunting, something that everyone in my rural community did, stories I remember were about bad weather, ornery cows, runaway horses, and bumbling city salesmen.

The vast majority of these stories were humorous, although the subjects and the situations were generally far from being funny. Humor was a way of making a bad situation better, and something good in something that was sometimes awful, and evoking laughter in a situation that was filled with tears. Stories about a farmstead fire, a charging mad bull, or a tipped-over pickup truck. Stories about minor and sometimes not-so-minor injuries caused by poor judgment or lack of knowledge.

Most communities—mine was one of them—had a storyteller adept at inventing facts and situations and weaving them into the most outrageous stories that most of us enjoyed, but almost all knew had not a smidgeon of truth in them. Of course, these "truth inventors" themselves became the subject of stories. "Did you hear the story that Bill told last week about the mountain lion he saw in his backyard?" Or some people merely dismissed Bill's stories, "You just can't believe a word that old Bill says. He's an out-and-out liar."

Humorous stories helped country people live through the tough times, when the rains didn't come and the crops dried up; when a friend or relative died; when milk prices fell; when someone in the family was injured. When there was a devastating fire. Humorous country stories were homemade; they were of the people. They came from the land. And although they may have evoked a belly laugh or sometimes only a chuckle, they cheered up people—and in most instances, the story, in addition to being funny, had a deeper meaning. A meaning that transcended the story. For country people, good weather nourished their crops; a good story nourished their souls.

I have told hundreds of stories by writing them and sharing them in my columns and books. I have also told many stories via television documentaries. For more than ten years, I have been telling stories by writing in them in books, and working with PBS Wisconsin to create hour-long documentaries based on my published books.

Lessons

- Stories help me recall the past, while opening a window to my future.
- A story is more than words. Our stories make us different from one another, yet tie us all together.
- Storytelling can change us forever. By telling and writing our stories, we can discover meaning in our lives without defining or describing what it is.
- Stories ground me, give me pleasure, and provide me a sense of purpose in my life. They help make me human.

Part V
Informal Education

Beginning in 1994, I left university teaching and began working as a full-time writer and part-time teacher.

CHAPTER 14
LIBRARIES AND THE INTERNET

We had few books at home when I was a kid, and the one-room country school that I attended had but four shelves of books located near the woodstove in the back of the schoolroom. As a lover of books since I learned to read, by fifth or sixth grade, I had read every book in the school's limited collection. And I wanted more. In those days, the Wild Rose library would not lend books to kids who lived outside the village. So I was stuck.

Mr. Roberts, owner of the Wild Rose Mercantile, knew about my love of books. In the basement of his store, where you could buy everything from four-buckle barn boots to groceries, Mr. Roberts offered a small collection of hard-cover books.

While my mother was busy grocery shopping, Mr. Roberts would take me down to his book collection and recommend books for me to buy. I saved my money from picking cucumbers, potatoes, and green beans—and I bought books. He showed me books he thought I'd like to read: *Swiss Family Robinson* by Johann Wyss, *Hans Brinker* by Mary Mapes Dodge, *The Black Arrow* by Robert Louis Stevenson, and more. They were 49 cents, in hardcover, and I have them on my shelf today. As I look back to those early days on the farm, and to Arnol Roberts' interest in helping me, I am so thankful for people like him.

One of the reasons I'm a writer is my great love for books. Today's libraries make them available to everyone. Over the past several years, I have spoken at 135 Wisconsin public libraries, from north to south in Wisconsin, from east to west, from the tiniest of the tiny to the biggest of the big. I shared information about my recently written books. In one year alone, I spoke at the Fitchburg, Shorewood (Milwaukee), Poynette, Frederic, Waupun, Plainfield, Reedsburg, Trempealeau, Wild Rose, Wisconsin Rapids, Boscobel, Mineral Point, Waupaca, Mt. Horeb, Green Bay, UW—Madison (Memorial), Park Falls, Brillion, Grafton, and Baraboo libraries. Each of these libraries, although many with challenging budgets, are vibrant places for learning and where the community can gather.

Every librarian I have talked to, and I've talked to many, say they have never been busier. Of course, like all of our public institutions, our libraries need our continued support, and for the "libraries are dead" folks—you are wrong. Communities love their libraries, and depend on them. It wasn't long ago that the word was out: public libraries will soon close. The internet will provide whatever it is you need to know. Libraries will join livery stables, ice boxes, and buggy whips as artifacts of history.

But as Mark Twain once said, "The reports of my death have been greatly exaggerated." This is certainly true for libraries, which are alive and well and booming in popularity. My hat is off to libraries. They are the community centers in many villages and cities, places where people gather, read books, and chat with each other.

Recently, I heard from Kent Barnard, the librarian at my hometown library, the Patterson Memorial Library in Wild Rose. The board voted to name a special section of the library the Jerry Apps Reading Room. What an honor. In addition to having several books of mine for checking out, the room also includes many of the awards I have received for my writing over the years.

Today, many of us take the Internet for granted, I especially value Google as a search engine to research ideas, people, histories, and more in minutes rather than in days, which was what I did before the Internet. The Internet began in the 1960s as a way for government researchers to share information. Computers were huge—I remember one entire floor of Sterling Hall at the

UW–Madison in the late 1950s and 1960ss devoted to one computer.

When I was in graduate school in the mid-1960s, I remember stopping at the Steenbock Library on the College of Agriculture and Life Sciences campus, and asking the librarian to check some facts for me on the computer. (The name of the college was changed from the College of Agriculture to the latter in 1967.) It was thought at the time that only librarians with special training would be able to search the Internet for information. Today, the Internet is available to anyone who has a smart phone, an electronic tablet, or a computer.

Beginning in the 1980s, email became a common way for communication between businesses, government, universities, and the military. By the 1990s, it became widely used by almost everybody.

Today, I depend on the Internet and its search engines for the answers to many of my research questions. Unfortunately, I have to be careful with the information that turns up. There are a goodly number of unscrupulous individuals and groups that use the Internet as a means of encouraging people to believe false information, and accept bogus conspiracy theories along with other dangerous activities.

Lessons

- Free access to books has been a key to my further learning.
- Libraries have provided me a source of information for my writing, and entertainment when I was not writing.
- The Internet is one of my important research sources.

I continue to enjoy and need the quiet of winter.

Chapter 15
Lessons From Nature

As a farm boy, growing up on a 160-acre farm in central Wisconsin during the Great Depression and World War II, I was immersed in nature. We lived a half mile from our nearest neighbor. We lived about a mile from the country school that I attended and walked there each day during the school year. Our farm home was adjacent to a 20-acre woodlot, where I spent lots of time as a kid, simply exploring, learning about nature without knowing I was doing it.

I was a shy little boy; when someone drove into our farm yard, I often ran to the woods, where I was safe. Where I was protected. Where no one would tickle me under the chin and say such dumb things as "You have really grown since last I saw you."

Often, on a Sunday afternoon, I would walk around our farm with Pa. In spring, we would look at the new growth in our woods, and Pa would say such things as, "It's time to plant corn when an oak tree's new leaves are the size of a squirrel's ear." It sounds a bit silly, but Pa was usually right. Pa studied nature the year around.

Walking in our woodlot, Pa would also say to me, "Listen for the whispers and look in the shadows." Look beyond the loud noises, and look beyond that which is brightly lighted. As I have lived my life, I learned that not only does that phrase help me see nature in-depth; it applies to my life generally. Listen to the people who are not yelling at me, but quietly speaking. Their wisdom may well exceed those who are yelling. And look beyond that which is easily seen in the bright light—look in the shadows. I have tried to follow that advice as I have lived my long life.

In summer, we'd walk along the farm fields, and check on the crops and how they were doing. But we also saw where rabbits lived in the fence rows where we had piled stones we had removed from the field. We saw bluebirds and meadowlarks and listened for their songs.

In the evening, when the chores were done and cows were let out to the night pasture, we looked at the sky and Pa told me what different kinds of clouds told us what weather might be coming. "Red sky at night, sailor's delight"—meaning no rain and good growing weather the following day. I felt the wind, and Pa would comment on how a north wind usually meant cooler temperatures. A southern wind meant warmer weather. Likewise, we'd look at the clouds at sunrise, "Red sky in the morning, sailors take warning." With that phase, Pa was predicting stormy weather for the coming day.

Canada geese have always interested me. I saw them flying over our farm in the spring and in the fall. I could usually hear them before I saw them. The Canada goose call is very distinctive, as are the Vs of them winging south each fall to return again in the spring. As a kid, on cool, clear fall days, I remember seeing long Vs of Canada geese stretching from one horizon to another.

Always curious, I did some checking as to why the Canada geese flew in long Vs. By following closely behind each other, the leading goose creates a slipstream, which helps pull the trailing birds forward. The lead goose also creates little pockets of spinning air, which help provide lift. Of course, the first goose in line benefits not at all from this, and has to work much harder than those coming behind.

When the lead goose gets tired, it falls back and another takes its place, and the flock continues on, honking happily as they look forward to a warm winter in the south. Geese prefer flying when the wind is down—understandable. It takes a lot of energy when there is no wind. It takes much more if the flock has to fly into a brisk wind.

On a windy day, the migrating flock will "layover" on an available body of water until the wind dies down. The pond at the farm we own now is sometimes a layover place. One day, I stopped by and saw the pond nearly filled with resting geese, each talking in its own way—no doubt grumbling that they had to interrupt their travels because of the wind. Geese that migrate over our farm follow the same "flyway" year after year. The route is familiar to them and they don't get lost in their migration.

Sometimes, I like to imagine what the geese are talking about when they are resting at our farm pond. Here is one of those times: I heard the familiar sound when I stepped outside the cabin for my morning walk. And then I saw the source, a pair of Canada geese winging over, just above the tree tops and calling loudly on this quiet, early morning.

I immediately wondered if these were the geese that had nested at my pond for the past several years, so I trudged off through my pine plantation, avoiding the several piles of squishy snow that remained in places shaded from the sun. As I approached the pond, still mostly ice-covered, but with a few feet of open water on the north end, I stopped, watched, and listened. I could see nothing until I caught some movement in the matted and dead grass around the pond—it was a goose, and then I saw the second one and they were walking toward the little open spot of water.

Once in the water they began talking to each other—a very different sound compared to the loud honking when they were flying over. I imaged the conversation between the pair went something like this:

"Look at all this ice, Mable. It's cold out there."

"For heaven's sake, Fred, don't you remember that you're wearing a goose-down vest?"

"Well, I'm still cold."

"You'll warm up when we start building a nest."

"Time for all of that again?"

"Yup, family comes first, you know."

Canada geese mate for life, different from wild ducks and many other wild creatures.

Here is another memory that is sad but so true. I was sitting at my pond on a frosty spring morning. The sun has been up for an hour or so. All was quiet and nothing was moving. A peaceful time. A time for deep thinking or no thinking at all. And then I heard it, coming from the south, the sound of geese flying. But the sound was not right. The usual call of geese flying this time of year was one of joy, at least it sounded that way to me. The geese are returning from their winter haunts to the North, to start new families, see old friends (I think that's what they do), and explore familiar territory.

The sound I heard was a sorrowful sound. Soon I heard its source, one lone Canada goose, flying low and calling a sound I've not heard before. The goose flew low over my pond, con-

For many years, I traveled to the Boundary Waters with my son Steve to experience nature while camping and canoeing.

LESSONS FROM NATURE

stantly calling. Has this lone goose lost its mate and is searching for it? Is this lone goose injured and not able to keep up with the rest of the flock, which has flown on without it? Soon the lone goose disappeared over the tree line to the north, and a bit later, the sound disappeared as well. As quiet returned to my pond, I continued to think about this lone Canada goose, calling so plaintively, and I wondered about its fate, as I wonder about all who are alone in this world.

Back when I was maybe ten years old, I remember one Saturday Pa asking me if I'd like to ride along with him to see a farmer on the other side of Plainfield. "Sure," I said. Saturday usually meant lots of work to do, and riding along with Pa seemed a great way to leave behind the several chores I ordinarily would have to do on a Saturday.

"The fellow has something I want you to see," Pa said.

"What?" I asked, always interested in stuff that Pa wanted me to see.

"It'll be a surprise," Pa said, smiling.

Now I was really curious, as I wondered what a farmer west of Plainfield would have that was different from what we had on our farm. Soon we were driving through the village of Plainfield and into farm country. Not long later, we pulled into a driveway of a farmstead, similar to many in the area. *Nothing special here*, I thought.

We got out of the car and the fellow Pa wanted to see came out of the house and began talking to Pa. I stayed near the car. I couldn't hear what they were talking about, but Pa motioned for me to come with them as they walked toward the corncrib. Seemed like an ordinary corncrib. We had one just like it at our farm.

The fellow pulled open the corn crib door and entered, with Pa and me following behind. Then I saw it, a big black crow sat on a little perch in the back of the corncrib. The farmer said to the crow, "Hello."

LESSONS FROM 90 YEARS OF LIVING

The crow, with a rather high-pitched voice, said, "Hello." Wow! A talking crow. Then the farmer said, "Jimmy Crow," And the crow said "Jimmy Crow." I had never seen anything like it—a crow speaking words I could understand. That is what Pa wanted me to see and hear. I've never forgotten the experience.

Many years later, I did some research on talking crows. One report I read said that a crow living in close company with humans can be taught to repeat as many as a 100 words and phrases. I was thoroughly impressed as I, at age ten or so, had seen probably a hundred or more crows, but never one that talked.

What is now the prairie on our current farm had been a cornfield in 1966 when we bought the place. Over the years, I have simply watched and waited to see what would happen to this once-cornfield if we simply left it alone.

Here is a little history. Thomas Stewart, a Civil War veteran from New York State, homesteaded our farm in 1867. He broke the land with oxen. At the time, it was a mixture of oak trees and open ground. The open area was largely made up of prairie grasses and wildflowers.. The land was stony, hilly, and sandy—far from ideal farm land. Homestead land was essentially free, 160 acres for someone willing to "prove up," meaning putting up some buildings and farming the land. Stewart sold the place after he had proved up, and a succession of farmers continued to work these sandy acres. They sometimes harvested a decent crop if the rains came at the right time, but mostly the crops were poor and making a living was tough.

My goal is to try to return this old cornfield into a prairie of wildflowers and native grasses. It takes patience but so far, outside of some mowing and keeping out the rogue trees and brush, I have done little to speed up the restoration.. It has been a joy, over these many years, to see how much Mother Nature can do to restore itself to what at one time had been.

I grew up on the home farm learning how to garden. During the challenging years of The Great Depression, we always had a big vegetable garden and depended on it for much of our food supply. Since 1961, when Ruth and I married, we have always grown a vegetable garden. Gardening is a wonderful way of being close to nature.

One of the crops that many people joke about is zucchini squash. Here is a fun piece about a more-than-successful zucchini I grew one year. Never had I seen such aggressiveness. Such a willingness to take over and be in charge. Such a show-off attitude. I'm talking about a zucchini plant that grew in my garden. I called her Harriet the Horrible. This was not an ordinary zucchini plant. I'd grown zucchini for many years. I've heard a litany of zucchini stories—I've got several of my own. These stories are all about the fruit of the zucchini—don't leave your car unlocked during zucchini season or you'll find a pile of them on the backseat—stories like that.

I'm not talking about what Harriet the Horrible produces. I would say she was average in that respect. I'm talking about Harriet herself. On the one hand, she was absolutely beautiful. She was six feet wide, four feet tall, and her leaves were more than 20 inches wide. Never have I grown such a fine specimen as Harriet. On the other hand, it's her personality that was in question, that is if you'll allow me to say a zucchini plant has a personality. She completely crowded out a cluster of carrots. She killed several onion plants. She has put fear and trepidation into four tomato plants that are scraggly and pitiful. She frightened the pole beans as they climbed ever farther up their poles, trying to escape the wrath of Harriet.

This was only August. What more damage could Harriet the Horrible do before frost comes and does her in? She was clearly on the prowl, holding her leaves high, and proudly doing what I have never seen a zucchini plant do. Harriet continued her mischief until October, when she succumbed to the first hard frost of the season.

I have always been interested in the weather, especially thunderstorms. Here is a memory I recalled about a thunderstorm, while I sat on the edge of my prairie one warm afternoon.

I watched the western sky as it turned from a hazy gray to the color of charcoal as the storm slowly organized and shifted east. It was a hot, steamy afternoon; temperature in the 90s and humidity not far behind. As the hours passed, the storm clouds continued moving, building, shifting, turning darker as they came closer. The air was thick and clammy; "Will it rain?" one of my kids asked, as the land thirsted for moisture after days of unrelenting heat and not a drop of rain.

Now the rolling, tumbling, ominous angry clouds obscured the sun and the afternoon grew dark and darker. I saw the first jagged flash of lightning and a few moments later, heard the grumble and growl of thunder. It had been weeks since I'd heard thunder and seen lightning—weeks of dry weather that turned green to brown. Another flash of lightning, another louder boom from the heavens and I felt the first drops of rain, as large as quarters splattering on the dry soil. And then more ear-shattering thunder and sky-splitting lightning and a deluge of water poured from the sky, cascading off the building roofs, running across the parched farm fields.. In its anger, the storm was giving up much needed, desperately needed rain. And then, after but a few minutes, it was over. The rain stopped. The skies cleared, and the countryside smelled sweet and clean.

* * *

When is a weed more than a weed? Yesterday, on my daily walk, I saw a huge burdock plant growing alongside the trail. Oh, how Pa despised burdocks. He placed that tall, "miserable weed," as he called it, right up there with bull thistles, which he hated with a passion. I stopped to look at the burdock plant (*Arctium*). Could it be as bad as Pa had me believing? I had watched him pull burdock burrs from our farm dog many times. He cussed the plant with every burr he pulled loose. I pulled a good many burdock burrs from my pants over the years as well. But as I looked at the plant, I wondered, *Could such an attractive plant be all bad?*

After a bit of research, I found some interesting information. First, burdock is native to both Asia and Europe and was accidently introduced to North America in the 1600s. Burdock is the inspiration for the hook-and-loop fastener, Velcro. According to what I read, a Swiss inventor, George de Mestral, in the early 1940s, was pulling burdock burrs from his dog, and he was struck by how well the burr worked—and voilà, he came up with the Velcro fastener.

Burdock historically has also served as a food—both roots and shoots are edible, as well as a medicine. In Asian cuisine, burdock root is usually sautéed in a pan with soy sauce and sesame seed. Burdock flowers and leaves and be used to make tea. The roots can also be used as a medicine. Supposedly, burdock root is a liver detoxifier, aids digestion, is anti-inflammatory, as well as being a diuretic and treatment for eczema. The lowly, often despised, burdock has an interesting, positive history—including the inspiration for Velcro that we all take for granted today.

Lessons

- I am a part of nature, not apart from it.
- Farms and farmers are closely tied to, and influenced by nature.
- Nature is filled with surprises; a talking crow is one of them.
- Nature is not in a hurry.

Lessons from 90 Years of Living

This maple tree was a gift for my 60th birthday.
I have enjoyed watching it grow as my grandson, Josh, has grown.

Chapter 16
Trees I have known

A tree is a tree, is a tree. Yes, but let's also consider that trees have personalities like so many other living creatures. Thus they may all be trees, but they are also different from one another. Take the white pine, the tree that graced the northern regions of Wisconsin before the loggers arrived. The white pine has long, soft needles, five of them in a cluster. It grows tall and makes a majestic statement on a landscape. I have about five acres of them at Roshara, all self-seeded, growing in what once had been a corn field in the 1950s and before.

The red pine—or Norway pine. as it is sometimes called—has two long needles in a cluster, is less graceful, but will grow many inches a year on the worst possible soil. I've planted several thousand of them on my farm. They are not as graceful as the white pine but they, too make a statement.

The jack pine is scraggly with branches that grow this way and that. It is the toughest of the conifers that grow on my farm-- a survivor of frigid winters and dry hot summers. I have considerable respect for this native tree. It may lack the grace and beauty of red and white pines, but it makes up for that in its toughness and ability to grow where other pines may struggle.

The white oaks that grow in my oak woodlot are tall and strong and powerful to look at it. Their soft gray bark contrasts with the deep furrowed bark of the black oaks. Even in winter, when their leaves are down, white oaks are a sight to behold, offering a dominant presence in my woodlot. The black oaks are common in my woodlot; they grow on the hillsides, in the valleys, almost everywhere in the woodlot.

But of all the trees that grow at Roshara, I am most impressed with the bur oak (sometimes spelled "burr"). I respect the bur oak's toughness. Bur oaks withstand fire, storms, dry weather, wet weather—they come through it all and continue living and growing year after year, sometimes living two or three hundred years. Bur oaks are not especially attractive when compared to some other trees such as a white pine, but in their own way, with their thick, corky bark and scraggly limbs going this way and that, they have a beauty all their own. Besides, bur oak trees are native to my farm. No one hauled them in from somewhere else. They have thrived in much of central and southwestern Wisconsin as long as anything living has been here. I marvel at that.

Some bur oak facts: They may grow 80 feet tall, even taller in richer soils, and reach diameters greater than four feet. The bur oak roots may reach depths of 20 feet and a lateral spread of 40 feet. The weight of the roots can equal that of the top. One of the reasons the bur oak lives so long and does so well is its tremendous root system—what you see of the tree is only about half of it—the other half is below ground.

I have a few trees that are a nuisance and have interfering personalities. They want to take over Roshara and have an attitude that suggests they are more important than their cousins. Black locust and box elder quickly come to mind.

What fun it is, at least for me, to think about all the different kinds of trees that grow at Roshara and how they manage to live together and mostly get along with each other.

Two trees, different as different can be, stand 100 feet from each other in front of my cabin at Roshara. They are both tall and they each have a story to tell, but that's about it for similarities. One is a balsam fir, the other an ornamental maple. The balsam fir's story begins in 1972 at Pine Point Resort on Lake George east of Rhinelander. That year, I was teaching creative writing at the School of the Arts in Rhinelander. We rented a little cabin at the Resort, and Ruth and our three little kids enjoyed the resort while I was teaching. Susan, then ten years old, found several little trees growing back of our cabin. They apparently had self-seeded. Sue asked the resort owner what kind of trees these were, and he replied, "Balsam fir." Sue asked if she could have one of the little trees, they were probably six inches tall at the time. "Sure," the resort owner, answered.

I helped Sue dig up the little tree and wrap the roots in some wet newspaper. We hauled the little tree back to Madison, where we planted it in our backyard. A couple of years later, we transplanted the tree at Roshara. It is the only balsam fir among the thousands of trees that grow at my farm. Now many years later, this little fir has grown into a tall, beautiful tree.

On my 60th birthday, my three kids surprised me with a beautiful ornamental maple tree, which was about ten feet tall when they planted it. It grew rapidly. But alas, in about its third year at Roshara, a buck deer, anxious to polish his horns, found the maple and stripped off a huge hunk of bark, nearly killing it. But it lived, and now it puts on quite the show each fall with its brilliant crimson leaves. Not to go too far with this analogy, but as different as these two trees are and as close as they are together, they appear to be getting along just fine with each other..

I like trees, all kinds of trees. Pine trees and oak trees, trees I've planted and trees that have been on my farm for a hundred years and more. I have learned much from them as I've observed them over the years.

Lessons

- Trees are like people. What you don't see about them is often more important than what you do see.
- Different kinds of trees know how to get along with each other.

Grandsons Josh and Ben help out in the garden, which has been an important way to learn about food and caring for the environment.

CHAPTER 17
SEASONAL CHANGE

I have always enjoyed seasonal change in Wisconsin, especially at my Roshara farm where a considerable variety of trees grow, many with a special color for each season. The coming of fall is a time for celebration. A time for thinking back to the season just passed. At my Roshara cabin recently, I wrote these words as the late summer days slowly turned toward fall:

> *During these last days of summer, the prairie at Roshara is a panorama of yellow with a sprinkling of purple accent. Goldenrods provide the yellow; blazing star wild flowers offer the purple. Honeybees are everywhere, working on the goldenrods, gathering nectar for what must be a delightful goldenrod honey. And the sometimes scarce Monarch butterflies flit here and there by the dozens.*
>
> *On a steep prairie hillside, the big bluestem grass, several large areas of it, is now six feet tall with its flowers spread wide—in the shape of a turkey's foot, as the grass is sometimes called. A few hundred yards to the north, in the deep woods, a maple tree's leaves have turned a brilliant red. Soon hundreds of other maples will join the aspen, birch and oak in a blast of color that will convert my woodlot from its many shades of green to reds, yellows, tans and brown.*

Lessons from 90 Years of Living

A few weeks later, I wrote:

The sounds of fall. Mysterious, interesting, sometimes even mythical. The calling of Canada geese winging south from their summer home in the far north. The "rat-tat-tat" of a pileated woodpecker chiseling a hole in a dead white pine. The barking of a gray squirrel from the top of a naked black oak. The call of an owl echoing through the darkness on a quiet October evening, then its call returned—a late evening conversation between creatures of the night. The sound of wind moaning through the tops of bare-branched oak trees on a windy day; the next day, in the same oak woods, the wind has gone down—the sound of silence. Memories of the sounds of the old Aermotor windmill on the home farm, and how on the nights around Halloween when the wind was up just a bit, the old windmill squeaked and squawked and tried to turn, but its brake would not let it. In my upstairs bedroom I could hear the noise and envisioned ghosts and goblins and creatures of the nether world on their way to visit me.

The other night when the moon was up and the wind was down, he came visiting for the first time this autumn season. When I was a kid, we called him Jack Frost who, with his magical brush, painted roof tops and grassy areas with a sparkling sheen of white frost. Annoying to some who wanted him to remain north at least until the end of the month, but welcomed by others who have waited for the heat and humidity of summer to sink south and leave us alone for a few months. As to damage, so far, just a grape leaf here and there that is crinkled and dead—and exposing more bunches of Concord grapes that I missed with the first picking.
 Now I look forward to one of my favorite times of the year, cool mornings with bright sunny days while I dig my potatoes, discover the onions I previously couldn't find, load up

Seasonal Change

the pumpkins and squash, husk the Indian corn with its many surprising colors, and enjoy sitting by my old woodstove on a cool, clear, autumn day.

A few weeks later, I wrote:

A late fall sun slowly crept over the eastern horizon. The thermometer reported eight degrees this morning as I made my way from the bedroom to the woodstove that provides most of the heat for our cabin. With some crumpled-up newspaper, a couple sticks of cured split oak wood, and the magic of some commercial fire starter, the old stove sputtered to life. Looking out the cabin window to a newly piled stack of firewood, now a little snow covered, I thought about my days on the farm as a kid. This time of the year and on into the "just around the corner" winter season, we began to relax a bit. The haymows in the barn were stacked high with alfalfa, clover, and brome grass hay. The corn crib was filled to running over with yellow cob corn. Our wooden stave silo was filled with corn silage, and the oat bins in the granary sagged from the season's annual threshing. The woodpile stood ready for the long, cold winter ahead.

As I looked out the window at a chilly landscape, I thought about how much the winter season drove everything that we did on the farm. All of the work from spring to fall centered on preparations for winter. For providing sufficient shelter and feed for the farm animals. And making sure the family had shelter and food to last until spring.

Frost covers everything: the lawn, the woodshed roof, the cabin roof as I start my pre-dawn hike. It is quiet, so quiet in the woods north of the cabin. No sound except for the crunch of fallen leaves as I slowly move along, listening, looking—the oaks are about one-third full color, the maples at peak color. I smell the wonderful aroma of fall—so different from the smells of all the other seasons. Pungent, earthy smells recording the hand-off of fall to winter.

As I hike back toward the cabin, the sun begins to peek above my neighbor's pine plantation to the east and soon I see the first rays of sunlight reflecting off the top of the big maple tree in front of the cabin. This tree, a gift from my children on my 60th birthday, shows russet red from top to bottom. A stunning display. Spears of green winter wheat contrast with the white frost in the garden spot—now tucked in for the winter with its green quilted cover.

And then it was winter. The long winter in the north is settling in, allowing time for resting, rejuvenating. remembering, contemplating—but mostly enjoying. Winter is for slowing down.

I'm at my farm these waning days of winter. The snow is piled high around the buildings, as high as I can remember. It took me more than two hours with my tractor to plow out my driveway after the most recent snowstorm.

I watched a deer last night, a little doe with a thick coat of fur. She was feeding on the brush growing under the windbreak not 20 yards from the cabin. Although she was up to her belly in deep snow, she appeared healthy. Even with deep snow, she appeared to move easily, albeit very slowly.

This morning, as the late February sun begins to crawl above the horizon to the east, I pull on my parka and head for the woodshed, a several-times-a-day task in winter, as my wood stove has a never-ending appetite. The thermometer reads 15 degrees. What I notice these chilly late winter mornings is the quiet—oh so quiet. The only sound is that of my boots creaking on the snow. I stop and listen to the silence—a real treat as most of my life is filled with sound.

The most striking and impressive sound of winter is the sound of silence. In winter, the birdsong and animal chattering and fluttering of leaves has ceased. On a windless day, there is often no sound at all. I may not have understood the power of silence in those days, but I do today, when it is more difficult to find than when I was a kid.

After nearly a month of below-freezing temperatures, the other morning, I woke up to the sound of melt water dripping from the roof. The ice was melting, the snow was settling, and a dense fog rolled in to make travel challenging. Old Man Winter was taking a break, regrouping for the next bit of excitement he planned to toss our way as slowly we turn our way toward spring.

This brief break in winter reminds me that not even nature charges ahead with all its fury all the time. We can learn a lesson here—especially those of us who don't know the importance of slowing down from time to time in our quest for whatever we are questing. We can learn from nature's example—take a time-out to reconsider, regroup, reflect, or read a good book and relax—before jumping back on the relentless treadmill that defines so many of our lives these days.

It is many years ago. My two brothers and I are in the upstairs bedroom of our old farm house. It has been a long, cold winter, with many below-zero days and snow so deep the old timers said they couldn't remember ever seeing such a tough winter. But something is different this morning. The most obvious—the bedroom isn't so cold. The thick frost that has covered the inside of the windows since last November is melting, puddling on the window sills.

Rain is splashing against the windows, one of the first sounds of spring. I look out toward our snow-covered fields to the east and I see wisps of fog. I pull on my clothes, rush downstairs, grab my barn lantern and trot to the barn. For the first time in weeks, the snow is mushy underfoot. And the subtle smell of spring is in the air.

Once in the barn for the morning milking, I notice the animals are aware of the weather change as well. They are restless and wanting to go outside, understandable after being cooped up in the barn for these long winter months.

After breakfast, we let the cows outside to romp in the barnyard, to run with their tails in the air, to experience spring. To feel the rain on their backs and the soft snow underfoot. But winter doesn't give up easily. That evening, the rain changes to snow as winter refuses to leave quietly. But we now know that spring is waiting in the wings, waiting for a chance to sneak in and take over, and push winter farther north for a few months.

Spring is in the air. I can smell it. I can hear it. I heard a robin singing this morning—no worms yet for this early bird—but it's here, its feathers fluffed with the cold, its song clear and strong. And the striking red cardinals are whistling their hearts out, happy about the coming of spring.

The sound of spring I remember most is that of melt water trickling through a stone pile in a gully in the big field just north of our old farm house. On a snow-melting day, I'd mush my way out to the field—sometimes with Pa, sometimes alone—and just stand there, listening. It was a tinkling sound, like that of a breeze teasing a glass chandelier. Subtle but definite. A sure sign that spring was just around the corner, although we often couldn't yet see the corner.

After a few days of dreary, bleak, and mostly colorless days in April, a few warm days in May change the landscape to a world of green. We celebrate fall for its palette of vivid colors, but if we want to see green—early spring is the season to see it. From the light greens of the aspen trees, to the dark greens of the white and red pine. From the reddish green of the maples to the yellowish green of the little nubs of oak leaves just pushing forth. Alfalfa fields, winter wheat, rye, and pasture grass wake up from a long winter. All green in various shades.

Lessons

- I enjoy the rich, earthy smells and sounds of fall.
- The quiet of winter has become an important part of who I am.
- Winter is for slowing down, resting, thinking, enjoying.

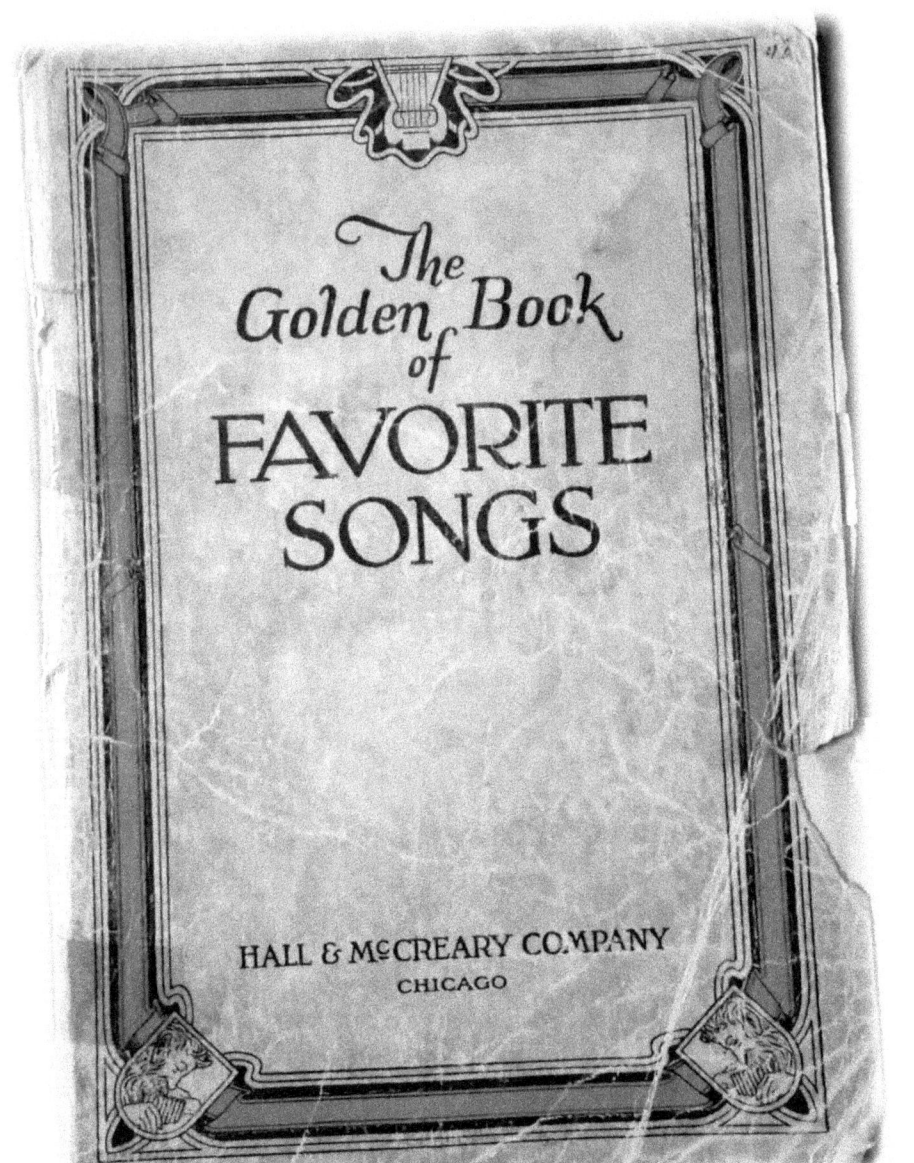

CHAPTER 18
MUSIC AND MOVIES

Three-Piece Farmer Band

Our farm community had a three-piece farmer band. The band consisted of Frank Kolka, of Bohemian background, who played a button concertina, Pinky Esherhut, German background, who strummed on a banjo, and Harry Banks, an Englishman who sawed on a fiddle. Not one of them could read a note of music.

During the years of the Great Depression and World War II, when times were tough and there was little laughter, this little farmer band played at birthday parties, anniversaries, wedding receptions, and whenever something needed celebrating. They added joy to a joyless time. Their playing confronted misery and put it at bay, at least for a few hours while people listened, danced, and enjoyed polkas, old-time waltzes, and especially Frank Kolka's haunting Czech folk music.

As a little kid, along with all the other kids in the community, I enjoyed the music as well. It was different from what we occasionally heard on our battery radio. And it was so very special—more special than I ever realized at the time.

Now many years later, I realize how important music can be to lighten the lives of people, no matter what their circumstances. I don't know if our little farmer band knew how important they were to our community of farmers, all trying desperately to make it through the Depression and World War II. But I believe they did know, for as they played, they were smiling, as making music surely enhanced their lives as well.

Lessons from 90 Years of Living

Music at the Country School

As I think back to those days so long ago, I realize how music was essential to a good life, especially when times were tough and there was little happiness or joy. Even though our one-room school did not have electricity during the early years that I attended, we did have a battery-operated radio. One of the programs we listened to, broadcast from WHA in Madison, was "Let's Sing," conducted by Professor Gordon. He was teaching one-room school students throughout the state how to sing—and what fun it was. Once a week, we turned on the radio for the program. Through the mail, Professor Gordon sent us music and words to sing, and that's what we attempted to do. Once a year, Professor Gordon invited all of his "music students" to Madison, to the University of Wisconsin–Madison's College of Agriculture Stock Pavilion, where we could see Professor Gordon and sing together the songs we had been learning during the school years.

Music had other purposes at our one-room country school. In addition to a battery-operated radio, we had a wind-up record player—a Victrola. On below-zero mornings in winter, when the school room was so cold we couldn't sit in our seats, our teacher put a John Phillip Sousa march record on the record player and all of us would march around the school room. I thought it was kind of silly, until I realized that the reason we were doing it was to warm up enough so we could return to our regular seats

Free Show Night

For many years, Tuesday night was free show night in Wild Rose. The outdoor movies began after Memorial Day and continued until Labor Day. We'd make sure to finish the milking early on Tuesday evenings. After the cows were let out to night pasture, we'd change our clothes and the five of us piled into our 1936 Plymouth for the four-and-a-half mile ride to town. My brothers and I received an allowance of ten cents a week, five cents on Tuesday and five cents on Saturday. For five cents, I could buy a double-dip ice cream cone, a big bag of popcorn, a Hershey candy bar or five sticks of Wrigley's spearmint gum. We usually got to town early enough to have an opportunity to spend our nickels.

As darkness approached and the street lights on Main Street came on, we settled onto the oak plank seats that stretched from Main Street along a little side hill on the banks of the millpond. A bed sheet was fastened to a pair of wooden two-by-fours, which were nailed to a giant willow tree growing on the edge of the mill pond.

We knew the movie was about to start when "Specks" Murty, the village marshal, arrived and let down the street light in back of the oak seats, screwed loose the bulb, and pulled the light socket back in place. The projector was an enormous contraption, hauled from town to town in a green, two-wheeled trailer. For years, the projector was owned and operated by the county superintendent of schools. It was his summer job going from village to village in the area with the movie projector.

Village business establishments paid for the movies: Colligan Auto Sales, Heuer's Meat Market, Dopp's Dry Goods, Wild Rose Mercantile, and so on. When we saw the names of the sponsors on the screen, we knew that in a few minutes the show would begin. A few of the braver kids held up fingers in front of the light so rabbit ears appeared on the screen. But we boys knew that if we did something like this, we'd catch the dickens from Pa and probably be docked our nickel allowance.

A serial—meaning it continued from week to week—played for the first fifteen minutes. The serial always ended with the hero facing a consequence so horrific we all wondered if he or she would survive. Of course, that was the idea so we would make sure to attend the show the following week.

After the serial, we settled in for the main feature, usually a Western with Gene Autry or Tom Mix or other actors we'd not heard of. In the background, we could hear frogs calling from the millpond, and often across the pond, we'd hear a whip-poor-will calling its name over and over. We'd arrive home around 10 o'clock, way past our bedtime. But no one wanted to miss the free show on Tuesday night. The experience added a dimension to our lives that was a wonderful contrast to never ending farm work.

Lessons

- Music can give joy during dreary times.
- You are never too old to experience the fun from singing.
- Music at the country school had many purposes.
- Free movies on Tuesday night added a new dimension to our young lives.

Part VI
Adjusting to Change

CHAPTER 19
RELIGION—BEFORE 1961

Religion is a difficult subject for me to talk about. I have several family members and friends who will have nothing to do with organized religion. I have also had my personal ups and downs with it as well. I am not alone. A September 2023 Gallop poll offered this information. More than half of the U.S. population, 53 percent, said they were spiritual but not religious, meaning they were not a part of any organized religious group, such as a church, Jewish temple, or a mosque. Eighteen percent said they were neither religious nor spiritual.[1]

Over the years, I have learned several important lessons from religion and from spirituality. First, here is some personal history. My mother, Eleanor Witt, was a devote Christian. As a child, she attended a German Lutheran Church near Wisconsin Rapids, Wisconsin, and a German church school. In each of these instances, everything was spoken in German.

The Witt family moved to the Wild Rose community when my mother was still a child. The family discovered, to their disappointment, that there was no German Lutheran Church within easy driving distance. After my mother and Pa were married in 1924, they occasionally attended a Norwegian Lutheran church located not far from our farm.

My father grew up in a family where religion was an on-and-off sort of thing. Before he was married to my mother—and I don't know for sure—he seldom attended any church. As a young child, I have no memories of ever going to a church, no matter what denomination. That is, until my twin brothers were born on

January 31, 1938. At that time, I was three and a half years old. When my little brother Donald became desperately ill the summer after he was born, my mother insisted that he be baptized. I had not been baptized—that summer, I turned four years old, full of questions and curiosity about almost everything.

My mother asked the Norwegian Lutheran pastor to come out to the farm and baptize the twins. I was there to watch in wonderment as to what baptism was all about. First off, the pastor asked for some water. We had no indoor plumbing so Pa got a pan of water from our water pail, which stood by the sink. The pastor called it holy water, and I wondered how the water became holy from the short trip from the water pail to where the pastor was going to baptism my brothers. I had earlier learned from Pa that there were times when I should keep my mouth shut. So I watched and listened as the pastor dribbled this now-designated Holy Water on my sick little brother's head, with some words that I don't remember. He then did the same with my brother, Darrel.

When the pastor finished baptizing my brothers, he turned and looked at me, standing nearby with my faced filled with curiosity and amazement at what I had just seen. He looked at me, and asked my mother, "Is he baptized?" Of course, the answer was "no." I then had water dribbled on my head as had been done with my brothers. I remember these words from the incantation. "Jerold is now a son of God."

How could that be? I wondered in amazement. I am the son of Herman and Eleanor Apps. How in the world can I also be the son of God? Again, I remembered Pa's message to keep my mouth shut in certain situations. This appeared to be one of them..

In 1941, a group of German Lutherans in and around Wild Rose built St. Paul's German Lutheran Church. Ernest Knoke, the owner of the sawmill in Wild Rose, was a major contributor to the project. Now my mother had her church, which we began attending more regularly. One of the services, as I recall, was in German, which made it even more appealing to the German speakers in our community. Pa could neither speak nor under-

RELIGION—BEFORE 1961

stand German, so he would only attend during the English services.

We only attended the West Holden Norwegian Lutheran Church for funerals, weddings, and various types of celebrations. Neither West Holden nor St. Paul's Luther Church had a Sunday school for young people, so during my growing-up years, when I was filled with church-related questions, there were no times when I could ask them. I didn't want to ask my mother; it didn't seem right that I should ask her those kinds of questions.

I have another memory, one of those events that likely had helped turn Pa off to religion. I was with him at a wood-sawing bee when the neighborhood farmers had gathered at Vilas Olson's farm to help him saw wood for his woodstoves, which we all had in those days. It must have been about 1946. When it was time for dinner, we all gathered in the Olson dining room to eat. The local Baptist pastor happened to be visiting the Olsons, and Vilas asked him if he would offer the noon prayer.

This was unusual, as I don't recall there was any meal praying at any of the neighborhood bees, whether it was threshing, silo filling, corn shredding, or wood sawing. He began praying and he continued praying. I watched the faces of the men around the table, hungry to eat the fine spread of food that Mrs. Olson had put before us. But he continued to pray and pray and pray some more. I don't remember the words he used, but there were a lot of them that continued to pour out of his mouth like a river spilling over its banks after a spring rain gusher. Finally, an "Amen" and we began to eat cold food and think nasty thoughts about the long-winded Baptist preacher. All Pa could talk about when we drove home that afternoon, was about the long-winded preacher praying and how there was no place for it at a wood-sawing dinner.

In the summer of 1947, the year I graduated from eighth grade, I was recovering from polio. I was 13 years old and a miserable kid, because at the beginning of summer, I was barely able to walk. I was only able to do limited chores around the farm, much to my disappointment and probably more so to my brothers, who had to do the work that I would ordinarily be doing.

I did not have a bicycle at the time; nor did any of the kids attending my country school. These were Depression and War years, and none of the farmers had any extra money for such things as bicycles. I had asked for one a couple of times, but Pa said "Nobody needs a bike—not when you are able to walk." I tried to remind him that I was just learning to walk again. But then, one a day in late May, Pa said, "How would you like to have a bike?"

"Sure," I quickly answered, wondering why this change of mind. He had noticed an ad in the *Waushara Argus* for a used bike for sale at a home in Pine River. On a Saturday morning, Pa and I got into the '36 Plymouth and drove to Pine River, which is located a few miles east of Wild Rose. We found the address, and saw the bike with shiny silver fenders standing outside a home. There was a For Sale attached to it. If I remember correctly, the price was ten dollars.

I was thrilled that I now had a bike, and a beauty it was. In those days, bikes were one speed. The bike had its problems, such as when going up a hill, the drive chain would slip, and if the hill was really steep, I had to walk with my bike. But these little problems I could put up with, as now I had a bike. As far as I knew, I was the only kid in the neighborhood who had one.

I soon learned why I had a bike. As I mentioned earlier, my mother was much more a religious person than Pa. Pa kept having these bad experiences, such as the one we had at Vilas Olson's wood sawing bee with the long-winded pastor. My mother wanted me to attend confirmation classes that would be held every morning during the summer of 1947 at St. Paul's Lutheran Church in Wild Rose, which was about four and a half miles from our farm. I was to ride my bike to Wild Rose five days a week in June and July.

My brothers were really upset, as I was going to get out of a half-day's summer work for two months. As it turned, out I would have rather been doing farm work than attending the confirmation classes, but following Pa's earlier advice, I didn't complain. This was something my mother wanted me to do, so I did it.

There were five of us in the confirmation class—three girls and two boys. I didn't know any of the other kids.. The German Lutheran pastor was in charge, and I soon learned that he wanted us all to pay attention to what he had to say, and under no circumstance should we say anything. He didn't say that in so many words, but we quickly knew that is what he meant. But curious me had to ask a question.. I held up my hand. As I think back at the situation now, the pastor probably thought I had to go to the bathroom. The church had indoor plumbing; at home we continued to visit the little house back of the big house.

But I didn't have to go to the bathroom. I asked, "Why does the Bible not have any new chapters? Everything in the Bible seems kind of old."

The look on the pastor's face was one of total disbelief. He asked me to repeat the question—I noticed that a couple of my fellow confirmands had begun to snicker. They knew, and I soon found out, that questions like the one I had just asked were totally inappropriate. Now I wondered that maybe God would send a bolt of lightning down and strike me dead. But no such thing happened.

I continued to memorize readings, ending with the words "This is most certainly true." I wanted to ask, "Why is this true? What makes it true?" And then a question followed the "most certainly true" with "What does this mean?" The answer was there, and we were supposed to memorize it.. Never once did I hear the pastor ask, "What does this statement mean to you?" I had some ideas, but I dared not share them.

I decided to do what the other kids were doing—memorize what we were supposed to memorize. At the end of the summer, at one of the regular church services, the five of us were quizzed on our knowledge as we stood in front of the congregation of

German Lutheran parishioners. The pastor asked us questions, and we repeated the answers we had memorized. We all passed, and were now confirmed members of St. Paul's Lutheran Church. We could take communion, the bread and wine, along with the rest of the adult church members.

On Communion Sundays, we stood in line to meet with the pastor, who asked us about what sins we may have committed the previous week. "None that I am aware of," was my usual answer. In truth, there were probably many.

That fall, I entered Wild Rose High School, and we more regularly attended church services at St. Paul's in Wild Rose. In the fall of 1951, when I had just turned 17, I was off to the University of Wisconsin in Madison. In addition to all the other adjustments I had to make, my mother insisted I find a German Lutheran Church to attend.

I discovered a Lutheran Church (not a German Lutheran Church) near campus and learned that they had a Sunday supper each week. These I began attending, mostly for the supper. But because I had little to no money, I got a job that meant I would be working on Saturdays and Sundays—so no more church suppers and no more church for almost all of my college years.

Because I had enrolled in Reserve Officer Training Corps (ROTC) classes for four years, I was now required to go on active duty in the U.S. Army after I graduated from the university.

I was stationed at Fort Eustis, Virginia. On occasion, I attended church services led by an Army chaplain. I found his sermons interesting and considerably different from my German Lutheran pastor, who never wavered from making sure he reminded each of us that we were sinners and in need of spiritual help.

I was part of a new Army Reserve plan for officers. Six months on active duty and six more years as a reservist. I returned to Madison and spent a year in graduate school, working on a master's degree. I don't recall going to church or being a part of any religious activity that year. I was very busy attending classes and working on my research project required for the degree.

This lesson I learned from my mother, without me even realizing I was learning it. Every night, when I was a little kid, when she tucked me into bed, she recited this little prayer: *Now I lay me down to sleep, I pray thee Lord my soul to keep; For if I die before I wake, I pray thee Lord my soul to take.*"

LESSONS:

- It is okay to be a doubter. When I doubt something, including religion, I usually learn something new.
- Religion is a difficult subject. Trained as a social scientist, I look for evidence when something new is presented to me. Depending on faith for the answer to some of my questions is a new idea for me.
- Organized religion (churches) takes many forms. Although believing in a God is foundational, the dogma of churches varies from almost total exclusionary to nearly totally inclusionary and open to all, no matter who they are, and where they have been in their lives.
- A church is much more than a building.
- We each have a spiritual self, along with a creative self and a critical self.
- I have learned to talk to God, something I do almost every day.

Our wedding day, May 20, 1961 at Hope Lutheran Church in Wautoma..

CHAPTER 20
RELIGION—AFTER 1961

In the spring of 1957, I began work in Green Lake County as a County Extension Agent for the College of Agriculture at UW–Madison. I had no church involvement.

All of that changed in 1959 when I met Ruth Olson, who worked in my home county of Waushara as an Extension Home Economist. I had been so busy for the past few years that I had little time for serious dating. And then I met Ruth. We were engaged on November 11, 1960 and married May 20, 1961, at Hope Lutheran Church in Wautoma.

A funny story that took place on the Saturday two weeks before our wedding. The pastor of Hope Lutheran had arranged for Ruth and me to meet with him to receive marriage counseling. When we arrived at his home a few minutes before the meeting time, his wife answered the knock on the door. When I explained why we were there, she said, "Oh, my gosh, he's gone fishing. This is opening day of fishing season you know. I am so sorry."

I mumbled something along the lines that I had planned to go fishing as well. And Ruth and I both laughed. I knew how important the opening day of fishing season was to Wisconsin people. Without marriage counseling, Ruth and I managed to be married 63 years.

Ruth came from a devoted Norwegian Lutheran family. Her parents both sang in the church choir and her mother served as head of the church Sunday school. I began attending church with Ruth. At first, I considered going to church because that is what I knew Ruth wanted me to do. Sort of like the situation between my mother and father. I was working in Green Bay, when we were married, and she joined me there. We found a Lutheran church in Green Bay, among the many Catholic churches that were there.

We moved to Madison in 1962, and became members of Midvale Community Lutheran Church. It was only two blocks from our home, and we always walked to church on Sunday morning. We continue as members of that church today. Along the way I changed my mind about churches. I served on the church council, was chairman of the adult education committee, ushered for 20 years, and eventually became president of the congregation.

As a result of these early church years at Midvale, I wrote two books about the experience: *How to Improve Adult Education in Your Church,* and *Ideas for Better Church Meetings*, both published by Augsburg Press. I also wrote articles for the *Lutheran Standard* magazine. One article I especially enjoyed writing was based on my years as an usher. In those days, when you arrived in church, an usher would ask "Where would you like to sit?" And then they would escort you to your seat.

The answer most people gave was, "About half way, please." It was impossible to do that after the first few dozen people were seated half way. The title of the piece that I wrote for the *Lutheran Standard* was, "About Half Way, Please."

In the mid-1960s, our country was in turmoil. Students and others were protesting the war in Viet Nam, those interested in improving the environment, including clean water and air, were protesting in the streets. Women's groups were protesting for their rights, and a powerful group was protesting civil rights for people of color.

As chairman of the newly organized adult education committee at Midvale Lutheran, I knew that several council members expected that I would organize Bible study groups. I could have done that, and it would have been appropriate. But I wanted to do something different. In 1964, I began my career as a professor at the University of Wisconsin–Madison. I suggested to the adult education committee that perhaps we might tackle some of the problems that society was facing. I was deeply involved with them at the university.

Most of the committee agreed with me. As chairman of the adult education committee, I was also a member of the church council, the decision-making group for the congregation. I presented the adult education's committee ideas for programming to the council. Some eyebrows rose, and one council member accused me of being a Communist for the ideas I had. Had it not been for then-Pastor Stan Klyve's support for our ideas, they would not have moved forward. "They are not church-related ideas" as that council member called them,

I first invited Fred Harvey Harrington, President of UW–Madison to speak at our first adult education session, which was held in the lower level of the church. I happened to know President Harrington, as he was a mild-manned history professor before becoming president of the UW. We had some common interests in Wisconsin history. When church members learned he was coming, they were aghast. Why would I invite the devil himself to speak at our church? Several of them said, "He has lost control of the students on the UW campus." True, many students were protesting, as was their right.

On the Sunday morning that President Harrington spoke, every chair in the room was filled, and people were standing in the back of the room. I had never seen a larger group at church for an "educational" session. President Harrington spoke for about 45 minutes, in the quiet, informative way that was his style. Several people later told me that he seemed like an ordinary guy. He was that. I don't know how many people changed their minds about student protests and the role of the university, but I suspected that several did.

The next Sunday, I invited Otto Festge to speak. At the time, he was Mayor of Madison. He was also a member of Midvale Lutheran Church and someone I knew well. Again the meeting room was full, as Otto explained what was going on in the city in the midst of so many protests both on and off campus. Many church members knew Otto, but I doubt they knew what his perspective was on what was going on in a Madison, and what he was doing about it.

Otto helped me get in touch with Madison's Chief of Police at the time, Wilbur Emory, and the following Sunday, he spoke on the topic of "What are the police doing about the protests in Madison?" Again, a full room and a most interesting discussion as the police had been accused of brutality in trying to control the protestors.

The next person I asked to speak, I'm sorry to say, caused more discussion from the adult education committee and from the church council than the others. Our adult education committee invited a Black Lutheran pastor from a church in Chicago to speak as part of our adult education series, and we also invited him to give a Sunday sermon to our congregation in the sanctuary. The discussion in our adult education committee ranged all the way from "Why did you invited him? to "Where will he stand when he preaches?"

Finally, the adult education committee and the church council gave us permission to ask the Chicago Black pastor to preach a sermon, but he couldn't speak from the pulpit. To this day, I couldn't figure out why where he spoke had become such an issue. The sanctuary was filled that morning. He gave us a thoughtful sermon, thanking us for inviting him and for being interested in his work in Chicago. I was pleased with the outcome. Not everyone was.

The benefits, if that is the right word, from our belonging to Midvale Community Lutheran Church are many. The church is a community, a group of people that we see every Sunday morning, and sometimes more often than that. Since May of 2022, Ruth and I lived in an assisted living facility in Madison, and thanks to present-day technology, we joined Sunday morning services on my computer. Pastor Ken Smith, our visitation pastor, stops by regularly to give communion and to share happenings at the church.

Today, many people belong to no organization, churches included. They miss the opportunity to hear a thoughtful message from the pastor each Sunday and a chance to sing hymns that may have been a part of their childhoods, as they are an inspiration to me. Participation in our church helped keep me grounded, especially during the years when I worked as an administrator at the University of Wisconsin and faced days that were often challenging and filled with problems.

Our three kids—Sue, Steve and Jeff—born a year apart, entered Sunday school, and as teenagers became active members of the church youth group. Ruth and I knew who their friends were, we knew the values held by their parents, and we knew what the church leaders were teaching them. Ruth and I firmly believe that the church was largely responsible for helping us raise teenagers during those often difficult growing-up years with few problems.

For many years, Ruth and I also belonged to a group made up of six couples who became our special church family. We met for birthday parties throughout the year, moving from home to home. It was always a potluck meal, with lots of fun discussion during and after we ate. The group always met at our home for a Christmas party. Now we are all in the autumn of our lives. Several of the group are in assisted-living facilities, and four members of the group have passed away. But the memories remain..

Unfortunately, today, there is so much division in our society, politically, and religiously. It is too bad that somehow we have forgotten that as a society we are all human beings, with needs and wants. Our church is trying to bring people back together, no matter what their background or religious beliefs might be. On the next page is the statement that is available for all to see from our church's weekly bulletin.

Lessons from 90 Years of Living

Midvale Community Lutheran Church welcomes all because Jesus welcomes all.
With you here, we are closer to who God is calling us to be.
If you've felt excluded or harmed in any way,
you are welcome here.
Your gender identity, gender expression, and sexual orientation are welcome here.
Your family, children, friends, and partner are welcome here.
Your abilities, culture, socioeconomic circumstances, race, and religious background are welcome here.
Here you will find an affirming community
committed to racial equity
and welcoming of all.
We strive for all people to experience God's abundance.
In Christ, you are loved.
Welcome!

Spirituality is a term often used by those today who have turned their back on churches and organized religion, but who believe in a higher power guiding their lives. I taught a philosophy course for many years at the UW–Madison. In the course, I said that we as human beings all have a critical self, a creative self, and a spiritual self. Each dimension makes an important contribution to who we are and how we lead our lives. Different from those who argue that spiritualty is separate from being the member of a church, I argue that spirituality is an important part of belonging to a church.

I also believe that those who have given up on organized religion, such as not belonging to a church, can also have a spiritual life. But they are missing the benefits of belonging to a group, helping each other, helping those in need outside the church, as well as being helped by others. There is considerable evidence that being alone, especially if you are an older person, has many detrimental outcomes. Being a part of a church group is one way of overcoming aloneness.

RELIGION—AFTER 1961

A decade ago, I would never have written this, but I am a firm believer in guardian angels. I have one—maybe more than one.

During the later years when I was teaching at the university, I was often asked to give keynote speeches at national education conferences, in places like Dallas, Los Angeles, Boston, San Francisco, and other places. I was scared out of my wits before each of those speeches. I would say a little prayer before each talk asking for God's help in minimally not making a fool of myself, and helping people think a little differently than they had thought before. And it worked.

My guardian angel also had a sense of humor, I believe. Before giving a speech to a thousand or more people in an audience from around the country, I especially wanted to do a good job. I remember it being in Dallas. I needed to stop at the restroom before I went on the stage. I hurried to a restroom, which, unfortunately, was the lady's restroom. A woman had just come out of a stall. She had a shocked look on her face and said, in too loud a voice, "What are you doing in here?"

I hurried outside and found the men's restroom. I surely lost all credibility with the shocked woman, who likely assumed that if the speaker is not bright enough to find the proper restroom, he would have little useful to say.

Another example of my guardian angel at work. I was working at my farm, and noticed that one of my hearing aids was no longer in my ear. I had just gotten the hearing aid, and it cost more than a thousand dollars. My farm includes 120 acres, with several miles of trails that I had traveled that particular morning. I didn't have a clue where I should look for a hearing aid that was about the size of a pencil eraser. I was about to drive my ATV into my shed, and for some reason looked down. And there it was. My lost hearing aid was on the ground in front of me. My guardian angel at work

Lessons

- Listen to your wife. I was not a church-going person before we were married. Since 1962, Ruth and I have belonged to Midvale Community Lutheran Church in Madison, WI.
- Taking a risk to suggest something new for my church resulted in a few bruises—I had never been called a communist before—but I became convinced that a church has a role in helping its members understand what is going on in the greater community, and the church has a role in helping solve societal problems.
- The importance of having a support group as one moves through life remains abundantly clear.
- Our church has been the anchor in my life, as I faced the joys, challenges, sorrows and hardships that go with living a long life.

Chapter 21
Life's Turning Points—The Early Years

We all have turning points in our lives, some are joyful, some less so, but quite easily adjusted to, and still others that are sad and take a long time to accept. Some have dramatic affects that continue to influence who we are and what we do throughout our entire lives. Here are some of the turning points in my life, and as I look back at them today, some lessons I have learned from them.

In 1947, as a freshman in high school, I could not participate in high school sports, especially baseball and basketball because I was recovering from polio, and learning how to walk again. Coach Paul Wright suggested I enroll in the typewriting class—which at the time was all girls. I reluctantly joined the class. I was a miserable kid at the time, feeling worthless because of my inability to do what other boys my age were able to do, such as play baseball. I discovered the typewriting class was also the staff for the high school's newspaper, *The Rosebud*. The typing class members were responsible for writing all the articles and producing each monthly edition on a hectograph machine.

A dramatic and long-lasting turning point in my life was polio, which I contacted in January of 1947. My right knee was paralyzed for several months. I was a miserable kid, with strong feelings of worthlessness. During the late spring and summer of 1947, I was learning to walk again. Pa served as my physical therapist by massaging my leg every evening with Watkin's Horse Liniment. The summer of 1947, I was teaching my 4-H

My 4-H calf, Stormy. He is one reason I was able to learn to walk again after having polio.

calf to lead—it could be said that as I was teaching my calf how to lead, he was teaching me how to walk. .

My writing, public speaking, and PBS Television careers are largely based on my having polio and thus my inability to play sports and do other things that required two good legs. (See my book, *Limping Through Life*, Wisconsin Historical Society Press,

LIFE'S TURNING POINTS—THE EARLY YEARS

for an in-depth account of my bout with polio and how it influenced my life, and continues to do so.)

A second major turning point occurred in 1961, when Ruth Olson and I married. Soon to follow were the births of our three children, Susan, Steven, and Jeffrey. The early to mid-60s were years of adjustment and challenge, as we had little money and we worked hard at raising our children. These were joyful changes.

I never wanted to be a professor. I did want to become a teacher, but a professor, no. I grew up with little and saw professors having backgrounds so different from me, that I never gave it a thought. When I was asked to fill in for a professor who was teaching temporarily in Brazil, I said "yes," I never dreamed this would turn into a full-time position, but it did. I taught undergraduate and graduate student classes at the UW-Madison for 30 years.

The day my parents had an auction and sold the home farm proved to be another major turning point in my life. I developed a deep love for the land, and with the drop of an auctioneer's gavel, everything changed.

The coming of spring meant the coming of farm auctions when I was a kid. There were many auctions as small family farms closed down, one after the other. It was a sad time in the country. In was also a sad time for the small villages that depended on these farms for their livelihood, especially after World War II, farming changed—tractors replaced horses, electricity replaced lamps and lanterns. "Get big or get out" was the message of the day. In the neighborhood where I grew up, there was a small family dairy farm about every half mile. I remember them well: Bill Miller, Allen Davis, Andrew Nelson, Griff Davis, Arlan Handrich, Joe Hudziak, Charlie George, Bill Witt (my grandfather), Frank Kolka, Jesse DeWitt, and McKinley Jenks were some of the closest neighbors.

On a chilly spring day, in 1965, Pa sold our small herd of registered Holsteins at an auction. It was a sad day, for Pa had worked hard since the 1920s to develop and improve his dairy herd. Now he saw them, one after the other, sold. That evening,

My parents, Herman and Eleanore Apps.

when I walked with Pa from the barn to the house, he was crying. I had never seen him cry before.

Pa and Ma lived on the home farm until 1973, when they had another auction. This time the farm machinery, household goods, and feed were sold. And the farm itself was sold—all 160 acres, including the farm buildings. The auction bill also noted a category for "Antiques and Collectibles." Most of these items the folks used every day; they were more than antiques to them. A Farmall H tractor was on the list. Also, several horse-drawn machines—a dump rake, a two-row corn planter, a potato digger, and a hay loader. I knew each item, knew it well, knew the stories connected to it.

It was a tough time, for me, for my brothers, and especially for Pa and Ma. Farming was so much more than making a living for them, it was a way of life. The farm auction closed the door on a way of living—so important, but too often ignored.

Ma passed away in April 1993, Pa in July 1993. At the time of their passing, I was 59 years old. Ma had fallen a couple years before her passing and broken her hip. As a result, she began suffering from severe dementia—to the point that the only other person she recognized was Pa. She was living in a nursing home and she believed I was her brother, Wilbur. Wilbur had passed away several years before she did. Visiting my mother, in her state of mind, was especially difficult for my brothers and me to adjust to.

Pa's mind stayed sharp up until he passed. When my mother passed in April, I had little time for grieving as I was national director of a program titled National Extension Leadership Development Program. What happened is my grieving process went on for several months, overlapping the grieving I did for Pa. who passed on the day before my 60th birthday.

I did a good bit of grieving at my farm, sitting on the banks of my pond, watching the water, listening to the birds sing, and thinking about my parents and all that I had learned from them over the years. In the early pages of this book, I shared some of the lessons I learned from them during my growing up years. Here are a few other lessons, also from my parents, that I have never forgotten:

Lessons

- Polio has long-term effects. Many things I can do. Many things I cannot.
- When one door closes, with the help of others, another door may open.
- Nothing is more important than family.
- Sometimes an unexpected opportunity appears. Take advantage of it.
- Lessons as a kid on the farm have been important to me for my entire life.

Notable Lessons from my Mother

- Don't brag. Let your actions speak louder than your words.

Lessons from 90 Years of Living

- Never do anything that will damage your name, for once your name is damaged, it will always be damaged.

Notable Lessons from my Father

- If you have nothing to say, please don't say it.
- Do the best you can with what you have.
- Listen for the whispers and look in the shadows.

CHAPTER 22
LIFE'S TURNING POINTS—THE LATER YEARS

Beyond my early and continuing problems with polio, my next major health challenge occurred when I was 86 years old. I retired from the university when I was 60. I continued to write books, do radio and television work, and gave as many as three talks a week related to my books.

In September of 2020, in the midst of the COVID pandemic, I noticed blood where it shouldn't be. I saw my doctor, who suggested it may be caused by a urinary infection. He gave me a prescription for an antibiotic and said I should see him again, if the blood persisted. It continued to appear, off and on, after the antibiotic treatment.

I had a CT scan on Oct.22, 2020. I then met with a urologist who said they had found something in the bottom of my bladder. The urologist suggested a cystoscopy to be done on November 10, 2020. Results of cystoscopy: a small tumor in my bladder, which required surgery to remove. The hospital was filled with COVID cases. No date was set for my surgery until January 4, 2021. The surgery was to take three to four hours. and could be outpatient if everything went well. On December 10, 2020, I developed a urinary infection. Antibiotics helped control it. But I was getting up three to four times a night to go to the bathroom.

On January 4, 2021, from 7:00 a.m. to 1:00 p.m., the surgery took place at St. Mary's Hospital to remove the tumor. There was no immediate word if it was cancerous. This was my first surgery, the first time I had been in a hospital. All seemed to be going well as I returned home and slept the rest of the day. On January 5th, I

The Apps family celebrating my 70th birthday at our farm. Back row (L to R): Sue, Ben, Josh, Steve, Natasha, Sandy, Jeff, Libby (baby). Front row (L to R): Jerry, Ruth, Nick, Christian.

learned the tumor was cancerous. It was determined to be stage 3 cancer, still confined to the bladder—a good thing. A follow-up surgery was set for February 15, 2021. The second surgery found no new cancer in or around the bladder. Good news. On February 25, I began six months of treatments with Bacillus Calmette-Guerin, commonly referred to as BCG. The purpose was to keep any new cancer from growing. Since then, every six months, I have a cancer checkup—so far, all clear.

In 2020, Ruth began experiencing severe pain in her right leg. An MRI disclosed a slipped disc in her back, which was crushing against a nerve causing the leg pain, which in turn caused an inability to walk. She was confined to a wheelchair. After a couple of falls, and hospital and rehab stays, it became clear that she could no longer live in our home, where we had lived for 50 years. Our daughter Sue began searching for an assisted living facility. She discovered Renaissance Senior Living at Hilldale, in Madison, Wisconsin. It opened on May 1, 2022. We moved in on May 4, 2022. Shortly after that, we contacted a realtor and sold our home.

Ruth and I were married in 1961 and had never lived in an apartment. We were now living in a third-floor apartment, with about the same square footage as our first home. Our new apartment included a small kitchenette, a large dining area, a small living room, two bedrooms, two bathrooms, and four closets. Management allowed me to convert one bedroom into an office, which turned out to be nearly the same size as the office I had in our home.

Cleaning out our home before moving became a major task. All three of our children and their spouses worked the better part of two weeks, sorting, sharing, tossing, reminiscing, and moving most of our furniture to our new apartment. This was a difficult time. Lots of memories were tied to our home. In many ways, after moving to our new apartment, I grieved the loss of our old home.

Once in our new apartment, we discovered that some personal adjustment was in order—in fact, lots of adjustment—especially for me as I missed my home office, the view of our backyard with the flowers, squirrels and birds, and my raised vegetable garden that provided tomatoes, green beans, cucumbers, and lettuce throughout the summer and early fall.

Nevertheless, an assisted living facility is where we needed to be, as now Ruth received the help she needed.

I was adjusting to my new office, which didn't take long. Ruth especially enjoyed eating in our resident dining room, not having to do any cooking, and took great pleasure meeting new friends. I, too, enjoyed the variety of meals and desserts that were offered to us each day, seven days a week. I liked to eat breakfast early, around 5:00 a.m., so I continued doing that in our kitchenette, where we had a refrigerator and a microwave. Ruth ate her breakfast in our apartment a couple of hours later.

I noticed that people who have lived by themselves before moving to Renaissance Senior Living appeared to have more difficulty adjusting to having other people around at meals, in the halls and elevators, and at the many events that Renaissance sponsored. One gentleman was a notable example. Ruth and I noticed that he always sat alone at his meals, so one day, we decided to sit with him. The dining room has tables for four people. "How's it going?" I asked the fellow when we sat down, and introduced ourselves.

"Not good," he grumbled. "I hate this place. I wanna go home." We learned that the fellow's grown children had sold his house and his car. He had no home to return to. We continued to eat with him as he slowly mellowed and adjusted to assisted living. We considered it a minor victory when one day he even laughed at one of my lame jokes.

We have tried to help newcomers, especially those who have some difficulty adjusting to having people around after living alone for some time. We see the group as a community; we try to help people get acquainted with each other, and with the facilities here. One example. We have a delightful library at the Renaissance. But no one was using it. Indeed, most of the newcomers didn't even know we had a library.

One day, Ruth suggested that we should start a book club, similar to the one that she has belonged to for many years. Different from most book clubs, in Ruth's book club, a member reports on a book with discussion to follow. We followed that model with the Renaissance, inviting residents to share books that they had read. It began in August of 2023, and has met most Monday afternoons at 2:00 p.m. since. I have noticed that several people, who had not been reading books, are now doing so.

Several residents at Renaissance Senior Living are confined to wheelchairs, my wife included. From Ruth, I have learned some important lessons. Being confined to a wheelchair, after spending most of your life being mobile, takes considerable adjustment, both mentally and physically. My wife continued to adjust to being in wheelchair, but with fewer complaints as the months flew by. One of the residents, Andrea Harris, has been in a wheelchair since she was a child. I have learned much from her about caring for and relating to someone in a wheelchair. Many of the wheel-chair lessons I share are from Andrea.

People in our assisted living facility have led interesting lives. Some were born in foreign countries; some lived in big cities, such as Brooklyn, New York and Chicago. Some were teachers, some had office positions. Some had lived in the north, others in the south. One was born in Hawaii and witnessed the December 7, 1941 bombing that marked the beginning of World War II. Another had deep roots in Italian cooking. Each has a story to tell—and from them I have learned much.

I owned a car since I was 19 years old. A few months from my 90th birthday, I sold my Subaru Outback. I told people that selling my car was one of the birthday presents to myself. I had seen too many elderly people involved in car crashes, where they and often others were seriously injured. I didn't want to be one of them. Had we been living in a rural area, I likely would not have sold my car. But living in an urban setting such as Madison, other transportation is readily available.

Lessons

- It takes time to grieve the loss of a long-loved home.
- If you or your spouse (partner) have health challenges, don't wait too long to seek out a facility to help you.
- When someone uses a wheelchair due to a physical impairment, it does not mean they are also mentally impaired.
- When talking with someone in a wheelchair, don't force them to look up. Bend down so you can be at eye level with them.

Lessons from 90 Years of Living

- Don't touch a wheelchair occupant's wheelchair, the occupant/user, or attempt to push the wheelchair unless the person asks you to do it.
- Don't touch the wheelchair's occupant on the top of his or her head; keep your hands to yourself.
- Don't talk louder to a person in a wheelchair. Hearing is likely not their problem.
- When someone is in a wheelchair, don't stare at them.

CHAPTER 23
LIVING THROUGH LOSS

Of the many months that I have lived, December 2024 ranks as one of the worst. It was also one of the months in which I learned the most about myself. My wife Ruth passed away on Tuesday, December 3. Her passing came as a surprise, but not totally, as her health declined as she adjusted to growing older.

As I write this on Christmas Day, 2024, I am in the midst of grieving my severe loss. I haven't felt such a loss since my parents died—my mother in April 1993 and my father in July 1993. At that time, I was working at the University of Wisconsin–Madison and doing a good bit of traveling as part of a grant I had received from the Kellogg Foundation.

I shed many interior tears as I traveled to several places both inside and outside the United States. When I wasn't teaching or traveling, I drove to my farm in central Wisconsin, and sat on the shore of my pond, listening to the bird song, watching the breeze play with the smooth surface of the pond's water, and thinking about my parents, what they had meant to me, and what I had learned from them. It was a difficult time.

In the 1970s to the early1990s, I taught a philosophy of education course at the UW. To put the purpose of the course in everyday language, I was helping my graduate students discover who they were as teachers—what they believed about the basic nature of students, what they believed about knowledge and how it was obtained, what they believed about ethics (principles that guide action—what was right and what was wrong), and what they believed about aesthetics (the need for beauty in their lives, their students' lives, and in their work as teachers).

The class examined alternative beliefs and values, which caused many of them to reconsider their own beliefs and values. I discovered it was difficult for many of the students to leave behind what they had once believed and valued. These were ideas they had learned in childhood and had held for many years. I shared a belief that I acquired when I was a kid, and one I left behind several years ago. Growing up on a farm, the occasional hawk swept down and captured one of our chickens. My dad branded all hawks as chicken hawks and should be shot on sight. I later learned that there were several kinds of hawks; most of them never bothered any chickens. I left behind my mistaken belief about hawks.

In 1969, I learned about Dr. Elizabeth Kubler-Ross's book, *On Death and Dying,* (a 50th edition of the book was published in 2014). In her book, she described five stages of grief: Denial, Anger, Bargaining, Depression, and Acceptance. Kubler-Ross's original intent for developing the model was to describe the various phases a person with terminal illness experienced when facing their own death. The book was hugely popular, and the model was adapted to describe grief in general. (See the book list at the end of this chapter for further writings about the grieving process.)

I took the model a step further in my teaching. I suggested to my graduate students that leaving behind their outdated beliefs and values involved a grieving process—such as the one developed by Kubler-Ross. Many of my graduate students struggled as they left behind their old beliefs and values and adopted new ones. Understanding the grieving process helped.

As we move through life, we have many losses for which the grieving process may be applied—moving from the country to the city, selling one's long-time-owned home and moving into an assisted living facility—I've experienced these events, besides my wife's passing. Other examples include divorce, loss of a close friend, losing a job, death of parents and other family members, and the example mentioned above—leaving behind one's outdated ways of thinking.

Although the process appears to be a series of steps in order, beginning with Denial and ending with Acceptance, that is often not how it works. People may jump around, be in Denial for a while, and slip into Depression and then move back to Denial. Also, from my own experience, no two people face grief in the same way. I remember a bit of how I grieved when my parents died, both in 1993. I was stuck in Denial for some time. Although I accepted their deaths a long time ago, there is scarcely a day goes by that something happens, and I am reminded of one or both of them.

Grieving is an emotional, physical, and psychological process, meaning it affects not only our feelings but also our bodies and our minds as we experience loss. Spirituality can also be a significant part of the grieving process for many people, often providing comfort, and another way to confront difficult emotions and find hope for the future. Persons grieving often experience upset stomachs, sleep disruption, severe fatigue, headaches, tightness in their throats, changes in appetite, difficulty concentrating and more.

For those seeking more information about grieving, check Agrace (www.agrace.org). This organization has compiled a series of suggestions for those facing loss, including the loss of a spouse or other loved ones. And check the book list at the end of this chapter. The grieving process has become once again very personal for me as I face the death of my dear wife. Grieving can take a long time, and its various phases come, go, and return. I am working on it.

On November 12, 2024, I wrote in my journal, "Twelfth day that Ruth is in the hospital. Jeff is here from Colorado, and together with Steve and Sue, we are looking for possible hospice facilities for Ruth. She is 87 and has had a good life. She has helped so much in the raising of our family, with my writing, my teaching, and with the marketing of my books, and so much more over the years. What do you do when your wife is dying? I don't have an answer."

Here is what I wrote in my journal on November 19, "With hospice care, Ruth continues to improve. Today we talked about the Christmas letter that we together wrote each year—including what events should be discussed. She continues to have good days and bad days."

Thanksgiving, November 28, was a special day for Ruth—indeed for all of us. She got to sit in a chair and eat Thanksgiving dinner with our kids and their spouses. and with me. I wrote in my journal: "Ruth was smiling. There were many hugs as residents and staff greeted her. We also celebrated a belated birthday for son-in-law Paul, and a wedding anniversary for Steve and Natasha. Natasha brought a Christmas tree to her room, with many decorations. It had been a good day for Ruth, the best day in weeks. She was tired, but pleased.

Ruth and Jerry Apps, married for 63 years.

This is what I did at noon on Tuesday, December 3. I had been visiting her just before lunch time. When I left her room at noon, I remember saying. "See you at supper time." She replied with the same. Here is what I wrote in my journal on December 4. "Sad, sad, time. Ruth passed away yesterday, right after eating a big lunch. Shortly after I talked with her. A shock to us all, but not totally unexpected."

On December 5, I wrote in my journal: "Not easy adjusting to Ruth's passing. We had been together for 63 years—lots of adventures, lots of fun. Lots of hard work as well." On December 6, I wrote, "It's hard for me that Ruth is no longer here. She was the foundation for so much of my writing, teaching, speaking, and television work. Yesterday, as I was working, I wanted to show something to her. But she is not here—will not be here anymore."

On December 18, 2024, Ruth's funeral was held at Midvale Community Lutheran Church in Madison, a church we had attended since the fall of 1962. Some 200 people attended the reception, the funeral service, and the lunch that followed. It was both a joyous as well as a sad time as I was greeted by people Ruth and I had long known. Some of them I hadn't seen for many years—they all came to say their goodbyes to Ruth and wish my family and me their condolences.

Brief List of Books For Those Grieving

Devin, Megan. *It's Okay That You're Not Okay*, Sounds True Adult; 1st edition, 2017.

Hickman, Martha W., *Healing After Loss*. Avon, 1994, 2002.

Kessler, David. *Finding Meaning: The 6th Stage of Grief*, Scribner, 2019.

Kubler-Ross, Elisabeth. *On Death and Dying*, Scribner, 1969, 2019.

Rondo, Therese A. *How to Go on Living When Someone You Love Dies*, Echo Point Books & Media, 2023.

LESSONS LEARNED FROM 63 YEARS OF MARRIAGE

- I was not always right. Ruth was not always right. With discussion, we usually decided what was right.
- To work with Ruth as a team for my teaching, writing, and media work.
- To work as a team for the raising of our three children.
- To work together during difficult economic times, and appreciate what we had.
- To learn together from our many travels.
- To be alone with the memories of Ruth as a foundation for healing and going on living.
- To take care of myself, physically and emotionally, because I have many more lessons to learn and to share.

Epilogue

In 2002, Ruth and I started a tradition that continues to this day. When the tradition began, I was teaching a writing workshop at the School of the Arts in Rhinelander. After I retired from teaching that course, we invited our adult kids and their spouses to spend the week with us at a cottage on Lake George. We've continued the tradition, now meeting at a lake in the Waupaca Chain O' Lakes. In recent years, family members came to the lake from San Diego, San Francisco, Denver, Minneapolis, Avon, Colorado, Gunnison, Colorado, and Madison.

Each evening is a special event: birthdays, graduations, and anniversary celebrations. One evening was always creativity evening. One year, the creativity evening featured everyone sharing an "Old Timer" inspired by the sayings I included at the end of the weekly columns I was writing at the time. Here are some of them, written by my grandchildren:

- We all must become more comfortable with being uncomfortable.
- In these turbulent times, five letters to remember: R-E-L-A-X.
- I was addicted to the 'Hokey-pokey,' but then I turned myself around.
- Happiness takes time, so don't rush looking for it.
- The sun sets no matter if no one is watching.
- Everything is better at the lake.
- Prior proper planning prevents poor performance.
- Life is tricky so make sure you plan for some time at the lake.
- Never curse the rain, unless you live in a tent.
- A trip is measured in miles, but captured in memories.

Lessons from 90 Years of Living

The week at the lake continues. There is time to relax and unwind—waterski, swim, play cards—and mostly learn what we are doing with our lives. There is also a underlying theme to these gatherings—if someone is having some difficulty, job problems, health challenges, the family is there to help.

Words I Live By
- With many years feeling worthless after having polio, I continue to work toward believing in myself.
- We are never too old to learn something new.
- Critical and creative thinking are keys to a meaningful life.
- I keep in touch with nature. I am a part of it; it helps me live my life as I learn so much from it.
- Accept help when others offer it. Do not fear asking for help.
- I don't know where I am, if I don't where I've been.
- Learning who I am is one of life's major challenges.
- Learning to keep love foremost in my thoughts, while leaving hate behind.
- Learning to enjoy the little celebrations in life.

Other Important Lessons I Have Learned

* There is a time to hurry: And a time to slow down.
* A time for thinking: And a time for doing.
* A time to speak: And a time to listen.
* A time to share: And a time to care.
* A time to work: And a time to play.
* A time to remember: And a time to forget.
* A time to be alone: And a time to be with others.
* A time to forget: And a time to forgive.
* A time to accept: And a time to reject.
* A time to sing: And a time to dance.
* A time to give advice: And a time to take advice.
* A time to laugh: And a time to cry.

(In the style of Ecclesiastes 3:1-8)

Epilogue

I continue to think about lessons I have learned in 90 years of living.

Acknowledgements

Before her passing in December 2024, my wife Ruth, as she had previously done with my other books, offered her critique of an early draft of this book. Always helpful, sometimes disturbing, her critiques made my books better. I will so much miss these critiques as I continue writing.

Huge thanks to my deceased parents, Herman and Eleanor Apps. I learned so much from them without realizing I was learning.

Thank you to my twin brothers, Donald and Darrel Apps—much of what I learned on the farm I learned together with my brothers.

The late Faith Jenks, my 8th-grade teacher, helped me prepare for the 8th-grade county exams, when I was confined at home with polio.

Thank you, Paul Wright, one of my high school teachers who helped me through a period of worthlessness from polio, by showing me an alternative to playing sports, which I could not do.

Howard Sanstadt, *Waushara Argus* publisher, printed my early freelance columns, which got me started with freelance writing.

Professor Robert Gard, a teacher and published author, encouraged and helped me write and publish my first book, *The Land Still Lives* in 1970.

Thank you to those who recently taught me critical lessons—even an old timer can keep learning. I especially want to thank Andrea Harris for her comments about how to relate to people in wheelchairs. Colonel Donald Klimpel, U.S. Army retired, reviewed and commented on my Army chapters. Thank you, Don.

A special thank you to pastors Katie Baardseth, Blake Rohrer, and Chaplain Jim Hergenroether, who helped with the church chapters.

And lastly, I want to especially thank my three kids, Jeff, Steve, Susan, and daughter-in-Law Natasha Kassulke (co-author with me of the book *Planting an Idea*), who read and commented on several drafts of this book. A huge extra thank you to my daughter Susan, a published author and excellent editor, for making Chapter 23, "Living Through Loss," more readable.

Many others helped me with this book as well. Thanks to each of you.

And lastly, a special thank you to Kira Henschel of HenschelHAUS Publishing for agreeing to publish this book.

BOOKS BY JERRY APPS

Early Farm Life

The Land Still Lives. Wisconsin House, Wisconsin Historical Society Press, 1970, 2019.

Cabin in the Country. Argus. 1973 (out of print).

Village of Roses. Wild Rose Historical Society. 1973.

Barns of Wisconsin. Wisconsin Trails. 1977, Wisconsin Historical Society Press, 1995.

Barns of Wisconsin (Revised Edition) (*Places Along the Way*), Wisconsin Historical Society Press, 2010.

Mills of Wisconsin and the Midwest. Wisconsin Trails. 1980 (out of print).

Skiing Into Wisconsin. Pearl Win Publications. 1985. (out of print).

Breweries of Wisconsin. University of Wisconsin Press. 1992, 2005.

One-Room Country Schools. Amherst Press. 1996, Wisconsin Historical Society Press, 2015.

Wisconsin Traveler's Companion. Wisconsin Trails. 1997. (out of print).

Rural Wisdom. Amherst Press. 1997. (out of print).

Cheese: The Making of a Wisconsin Tradition. Amherst Press. 1998. University of Wisconsin Press, Revised Edition, 2020.

When Chores Were Done. Amherst Press. 1999.

Symbols: Viewing a Rural Past. Amherst Press. 1999. (out of print).

Humor From The Country. Amherst Press. 2001.

The People Came First - A History of Wisconsin Cooperative Extension. Cooperative Extension Publications. 2002.

Eat Rutabagas. Amherst Press. 2002. (children's picture book)

Stormy. Amherst Press. 2002. (children's picture book)

Ringlingville USA. Wisconsin Historical Society Press. 2004.

Every Farm Tells A Story. Voyageur Press. 2005. Fulcrum Publishing.

Country Ways and Country Days. Voyageur Press. 2005, Fulcrum Publishing.

Country Wisdom. Voyageur Press. 2005.

Tents, Tigers and the Ringling Brothers. Wisconsin Historical Society Press, 2006. (young adult)

Living a Country Year. Voyageur Press, 2007, Fulcrum Publishing

In a Pickle: A Family Farm Story. University of Wis. Press, 2007 (adult fiction)

Casper Jaggi: Master Swiss Cheese Maker. Wisconsin Historical Society Press, 2008.(young adult)

Old Farm: A History. Wisconsin Historical Society Press, 2008.

Blue Shadows Farm, University of Wisconsin Press, 2009 (adult fiction)

Horse Drawn Days: A Century of Farming With Horses. Wisconsin Historical Society Press, 2010.

The Travels of Increase Joseph. University of Wisconsin Press, 2010 (adult fiction)

Cranberry Red. University of Wisconsin Press, 2010. (adult fiction)

Campfires and Loon Calls. Fulcrum Publishing, 2011.

Garden Wisdom: Lessons from 60 Years of Gardening. Wisconsin Historical Society Press, 2012.

Rural Wit and Wisdom, Fulcrum Publishing, 2012.

Tamarack River Ghost. University of Wisconsin Press, 2012. (adult fiction)

Letters from Hillside Farm, Fulcrum Publishing, 2013. (young adult)

The Quiet Season. Wisconsin Historical Society Press, 2013.

BOOKS BY JERRY APPS

Limping through Life: A Farm Boy's Polio Memoir. Wisconsin Historical Society Press, 2013.

The Great Sand Fracas of Ames County, University of Wisconsin Press, 2014. (adult fiction)

Whispers and Shadows. Wisconsin Historical Society Press, 2015.

Wisconsin Agriculture: A History. Wisconsin Historical Society Press, 2015.

One Room Country Schools, Wisconsin Historical Society Press, 2015.

Telling your Story, Fulcrum Press, 2016.

Roshara Journal: Chronicling Four Seasons, Fifty Years, and 120 Acres, Wisconsin Historical Society Press, 2016.

Never Curse the Rain. Wisconsin Historical Society Press, 2017.

Old Farm Country Cookbook, Wisconsin Historical Society Press, 2017.

Cold As Thunder. University of Wisconsin Press, 2018 (adult fiction)

Simple Things: Lessons from the Family Farm. Wisconsin Historical Society Press, 2018.

The Civilian Conservation Corps in Wisconsin: Nature's Army at Work. Wisconsin Historical Society Press, 2019.

When the White Pine was King: A History of Lumberjacks, Log Drives, and Sawdust Cities in Wisconsin. Wisconsin Historical Press, 2020.

Cheese: The Making of a Wisconsin Tradition (2nd Edition), Wisconsin Historical Press, 2020.

The Old Timer Says: A Writing Journal. Wisconsin Historical Press, 2020.

The Wild Oak. Three Towers Press, 2021 (young adult)

Settlers Valley. University of Wisconsin Press, 2021. (adult fiction).

A Summer of Peas and Pickles. Three Towers Press, 2022. (young adult)

Meet Me on the Midway: A History of Wisconsin Fairs, Wisconsin Historical Press, 2022.

More than Words: A Memoir of a Writing Life. Wisconsin Historical Press, 2022.

Planting an Idea: A Guidebook to Critical and Creative Thinking About Environmental Problems. Fulcrum Publishing, 2023 (with Natasha Kusslke)

On Farms and Rural Communities: An Agricultural Ethic for the Future. Fulcrum Publishing, 2024.

Timber!: A Northwoods Story of Lumberjacks, Logging, and the Land, Susan Apps-Bodilly and Jerry Apps. Wisconsin Historical Society Press, 2024. (young adult)

Lunkers, Keepers, and Ones that Got Away: Fish Tales from Four Generations of Anglers. Wisconsin Historical Society Press

Books Related to Continuing Education

Toward a Working Philosophy of Adult Education. Syracuse U. 1973. (Out of print).

Tips For Article Writers. Wisconsin Regional Writers, 1973.(out of print).

Problems in Continuing Education. McGraw-Hill. 1980.

Problemas de La Educacion Permanente. Paidos Educador. Barcelona, 1983, 1994.

Problems in Continuing Education. Arabic Translation.

The Adult Learner on Campus. Follett. 1981.

Study Skills for Adults Returning to School. McGraw-Hill. 1978, 1981.

Improving Your Writing Skills. Follett. 1982.

How to Improve Adult Education in Your Church. Augsburg. 1972

Ideas For Better Church Meetings. Augsburg. 1975.

Books by Jerry Apps

Improving Practice in Continuing Education. Jossey-Bass (Simon & Schuster). 1985.

Higher Education in a Learning Society. Jossey-Bass (Simon & Schuster). 1988.

Study Skills For Today's College Student. McGraw-Hill. 1990.

Mastering the Teaching of Adults. Krieger. 1991.

Leadership for the Emerging Age. Jossey-Bass, 1994.

Teaching from the Heart. Krieger. 1996.

Once a Professor: A Memoir of Teaching in Turbulent Times. Wisconsin Historical Society Press. 2018.

Source Notes:

[1] http://news.gallup.com/poll/358364/religious-americans.aspx.)

www.ingramcontent.com/pod-product-compliance
Lightning Source LLC
Chambersburg PA
CBHW050031090426
42735CB00021B/3450